The Hidden Face
of Free Enterprise

The Strange Economics of the American Businessman

JOHN R. BUNTING

Vice President
Federal Reserve Bank of Philadelphia

GREENWOOD PRESS, PUBLISHERS
WESTPORT, CONNECTICUT

Library of Congress Cataloging in Publication Data

Bunting, John R.
    The hidden face of free enterprise.

    Reprint. Originally published: New York : McGraw-
Hill, c1964.
    Includes index.
    1. United States--Economic conditions--1945-   .
2. Corporations--United States.   I. Title.
[HC106.5.B814   1982]   330.973'092   81-13353
ISBN 0-313-23218-0 (lib. bdg.)   AACR2

Reprinted with the permission of McGraw-Hill Book
Company.

Reprinted in 1981 by Greenwood Press,
A division of Congressional Information Service, Inc.
88 Post Road West, Westport, Connecticut 06881

Printed in the United States of America

10 9 8 7 6 5 4 3 2 1

Foreword

For some years during the presidency of Harry S. Truman, I read quite thoroughly a weekly compendium of speeches by American business leaders. The leitmotiv of these speeches, remarkably sustained, was that the American economy was going to hell in a hack, to use the technical term; and in decisive measure because the system of free private enterprise was being tortured to death.

Then, as I gathered and analyzed reports of business plans for capital investment, I found that the investment was being increased to an extent quite comparable to that with which the ruination of the economy was being envisaged. And by these plans the same business leaders who were regularly proclaiming the impending doom of the economy were giving about the most impressive vote of confidence they could to its robust future.

It is such contradictory behavior on the part of American business leaders that John Bunting explores analytically in the first part of this remarkable volume about the economics of the American businessman. He traces the evolution of the American economy from the time when Adam Smith's "invisible hand" (working to make almost all of us serve the public interest under the impact of competition regardless of our inclinations) was a dominant operative force, to the present, when it is often left up to major business firms (and presumably trade unions, too) to apply in large measure their own restraints upon themselves, in the public interest. In this process he portrays vividly the emotional and intellectual struggle of the major corporate executive in shifting from a conception of his business world as one in which he is in large part a pawn of market forces, with his opportunities and responsibilities reduced accordingly, to a conception in which he is in imposing degree his own monitor.

The territory involved in making this analysis is as tough and thorny as it is fascinating. Most of those who follow Mr. Bunting as he bravely and very skillfully traverses it will, I am reasonably confident, find some things to quarrel with. I did. But I believe they will also recognize that they are sharing in a major contribution to the modernizing of conceptions essential to the successful handling of our current and prospective economic problems.

Beyond the tour de force I have indicated, Mr. Bunting deals with such major issues of our time as growth, automation, unemployment, the proper uses of fiscal and monetary policy, and the consequences of possible peace, not merely as they emerge in the economics of the businessman but as they emerge in the economics of the nation. Here he applies his great talents broadly as an economist of the first rank, operating from a vantage point (in the Federal Reserve Bank of Philadelphia) which gives him more contact with business realities than most economists have, but also leaves him enough detached to save him from getting the trees mixed up with the forest, or vice versa.

If you gather from what I have written that I think this book is eminently worth reading, you are absolutely right.

Dexter M. Keezer

Acknowledgments

Many expressions of gratitude are in order in connection with this modest offering. First, my thanks go to all the audiences of businessmen who have listened to me talk for the past ten years. It was their patience and generosity that gave me the experience and confidence to take a year and write this book without breaking stride in my main occupation at the Federal Reserve Bank of Philadelphia. At that Bank, I must pay tribute in particular to Edward A. Aff, Joseph R. Campbell, and Lawrence C. Murdoch. Everything here recorded has come up at one time or another in conversations with these gentlemen. Ed Aff, in addition to his other contributions, served as an unofficial editor for me. Also, Clay J. Anderson and Evan B. Alderfer, economic advisers to the Federal Reserve Bank of Philadelphia, provided many helpful comments.

Recognition goes also to Mrs. Doris Dinger, who kept the manuscript separate from all the other work we perform together, and who struggled through the various drafts necessary to get an end product.

Of course, such an undertaking could not have been consummated without the complete cooperation of my family. Robin Ann and John are a year ahead of me with the "new math" and I have a feeling I may never catch them. Wife

Jane took over my leaf-raking chores to the consternation of our neighbors.

Finally, I want to pay special tribute to President Karl R. Bopp and First Vice President Robert N. Hilkert of the Federal Reserve Bank of Philadelphia. Neither of these fine central bankers—and my immediate bosses—will have seen a word of this book before it is in print. Needless to say, some of that which is written could prove somewhat embarrassing to them. How they resisted the temptation to influence directly the writing of this book I will never know. That they did is something for which I will always be grateful.

J.R.B.

Contents

1

No Divine Sanction: An Introduction

This is a book about the economics of the American businessman. It is an effort to determine what the businessman really believes about the economic system he makes go, what he thinks about the big economic issues of our times, and where his basic attitudes may lead him in dealing with the big problems of the future.

The conventional approach to a book such as this one would be to select a random sample of businessmen and ply them with strategic questions, or to pore over the public pronouncements of business leaders and their appointed spokesmen, such as the National Association of Manufacturers, the Committee for Economic Development, and the National Industrial Conference Board. I decided against this approach. Why systematically substantiate what everyone knows? Business leaders in responses to formal questions stick to their last. They speak what others have labeled "a slogan-ridden, old-fashioned language of conservative cliché." They confirm their image at the expense of their more profound views. The impression they leave is almost a caricature.

I respect those who differ with me on this, but it is my view that the statistical approach in areas such as this only confirms what is already known or provides essentially trivial new information. Nor can I imagine the inner soul of the businessman bared by the organizations that speak for him on public issues. Others are welcome to the task of proceeding through equations and graphs to conclusions concerning the economics of the businessman.

At the outset, I confess that I have relied upon the businessman's casual remarks, his responses to serious questions when off guard, and my own intuition. I have abstained from following any systematic procedure in eliciting information. The only categoric statement I can make is that no businessman quoted in this book or used indirectly to substantiate my remarks knew that what he was saying would be used by me. For the most part, what I say reflects comments made over cocktails, in the club car, at a board meeting, on a convention, and so forth.

No doubt, in the course of writing this book I have imputed some views to businessmen that have never been enunciated clearly. I don't know which these are. What is said on the pages to follow represents the way the businessman comes through to me.

Many, many business leaders have not, or do not take, time to think about economics in the larger sense. Their economic views are so colored by self-interest that critical, clinical analysis is necessary to make much sense out of them. This book attempts such analysis. Of course, not all I heard appears here nor has it all been consciously weighed in arriving at conclusions. To some extent, I am presenting views of those businessmen whose comments intrigued me.

Needless to say, this approach means that the reader risks getting only the prejudices of the author. There is no way to keep from running such a risk. Even the most documented, footnoted, statistic-filled book may be terribly biased.

At times, in order to provide contrast it has been convenient for me to speak for the economist also. That this is dangerous goes without saying. Fine distinctions in this science have become the stock-in-trade. Refinements on refinements have evolved into a pointless battle of "one-upmanship" among some economic practitioners. Robert Heilbroner, in *The Worldly Philosophers,* observed: ". . . the temper of most contemporary economists tends to be unadventuresome and academic. . . . Perhaps it is evidence of an unwillingness to peer too closely into the dangerous possibilities of a time of great historic stress." If the hairsplitting is to come, so be it. I have attempted to speak for the main body of academic economic thought.

Perhaps it may comfort the reader somewhat to know that, as a vice president and economist at the Federal Reserve Bank of Philadelphia and lecturer in economics at Temple University, I have had the opportunity to meet and exchange confidences with many business leaders and economists. In the club car I have heard the fuzzy-minded, ivory-tower theorizing of the economist damned, and in the faculty lounge listened to colleagues berate the economic illiteracy of the businessman. I have given about a thousand speeches to business leaders since 1950, and listened to two or three times that number. I have interviewed businessmen and economists on about 75 television shows. In short, I have had the opportunity to come to know the businessman. If my statistical sample is not scientifically drawn, it is large; if I do not get to the truth, I have had the chance to try.

It may occur to the reader to ask why he should be interested in the economic views of the businessman. The businessman is not, after all, an economist, or a politician. Is what he believes about our economic system, and why, really so significant?

At a two-day meeting of economists held at Haverford College in the summer of 1963 one of the speakers announced to his colleagues that "what happened in America from 1941 through 1945 should have convinced businessmen once and for all that government spending and deficits can produce a business boom."

It seemed to me that he was missing a really vital point. During World War II it appeared reasonable to the businessman that Federal spending should be huge and that taxes would not be able to match expenditures. Since businessmen saw the appropriateness of this level of Federal spending it was not offset by a diminution in corporate enterprise. On the contrary, the flood of Federal dollars encouraged business spending and activity.

On the other hand, an increase in government spending and a deficit of similar magnitude in a different context would not produce the same result. The businessman's anxiety over the irresponsibility of government would cause such uneasiness that a consequent hesitancy in business activity would ensue and partially, at least, offset the impetus provided the economy by such spending. In other words, in the American economy the businessman is still of decisive importance. Government economic policy can be most effective when it is correct, and the business community is so convinced.

This means that what the businessman thinks about economic policy is important no matter how myth-laden his views may seem. In this I believe strongly. It is the overriding reason for this book.

Without wanting to appear to be reaching out for additional support for my conviction that the economics of the American businessman is a worthwhile subject, it is noteworthy that the late President, John F. Kennedy, called for a dialogue with the businessman. In his address at the June, 1962, commencement exercises at Yale, he said: "Discussion is essential, and I am hopeful that the debate of recent weeks, though up to now somewhat barren, may represent the start of a serious dialogue of the kind which has led in Europe to such fruitful collaboration among all the elements of economic society and to a decade of unrivaled economic progress."

An effective dialogue cannot occur until the parties are well known to each other. Economists are well known to the businessman. They teach him at college, make their views known to him later through writings and lectures. The businessman may justifiably complain that economists spend too much time talking to themselves; that their language is growing increasingly specialized, to the point where it is becoming a kind of ingroup officialese, confusing to outsiders. The businessman may complain, too, that economists are cultivating techniques to the point where the subject is becoming more and more fragmented and less related to what economics is really about. At least, economists' views are on record for those with the perseverance and perception to read them.

The businessman is not nearly so well known. In his executive years, when the businessman speaks on broad economic issues, it is as if he forgot everything he was taught about the subject at college. His economic model almost seems to pre-date Adam Smith. As a result, the suspicion has become general that the businessman acts on assumptions that are no longer true, that he is caught up in slogans he himself can hardly believe, and that somehow he had better bring his thinking and actions into line with new principles. Is this really true?

There is yet another reason for a book about the economics of the businessman. There is always danger in a subject such as economics becoming prescriptive, that its philosophers and textbook writers are establishing standards, norms, and methods unrelated to its practice. The businessman makes economics. His mergers, changed accounting methods, reactions to new tax laws, evolving relationship with the capital market, and routine daily practices give economics its meaning. There is, after all, *no divine sanction* in economics. Our business system is an instrument of the people who use it. If what is read and taught is different from what actually takes place, then there is danger of ending up with textbook economics quite separate and apart from the living thing.

That the businessman has his own brand of economics—and that it has not been done justice by the businessman himself—had occurred to me from time to time in the past. But I was reminded of it one evening on the train back to Philadelphia from New York. I was sitting with two other Philadelphians, one an economist with a large hard-goods producer, the other a business leader in the area.

My economist friend had just finished declaring how glad he was that what had happened to New York had not happened to Philadelphia. Then he entertained us with a recitation of the reasons usually given for New York's spectacular ascent while Philadelphia grew more slowly. The comparative depths of each harbor, the Erie Canal, freight differentials, distances from foreign ports, and so forth, all were recounted.

I nodded confirmation. It all seemed logical although not exactly convincing. The glazed eyes and impatient expression of our businessman friend indicated that he had heard it all before, too. I tried to change the subject. To my surprise he cut in on the economist, "I must disagree with you. The reasons you give are valid economically. They make good explanations after the fact. But they were not of decisive importance.

"Philadelphia and New York were similarly endowed with natural blessings making for great cities. Neither had a real strategic advantage. Philadelphia prospered first as the leading city in the new United States. Most of my reading suggests that people came to Penn's land in great number to find tolerance. The Quakers permitted more religious freedom than other settlers. Philadelphia was their port of entry for the Holy Experiment, and it grew larger than any other American city.

"After a while, however, Philadelphia society closed itself at the upper end. To receive full social acceptance family money had to be old and substantial, with most emphasis on the 'old.' New York society also admitted members on these criteria. But in New York if you had *enough* money, you didn't have to wait in line very long. Its social upper end stayed open.

"As a consequence, ambitious, talented people gravitated toward New York and away from Philadelphia. They could go as far as their talents would take them and get full satisfaction there. In Philadelphia, business success went socially unrewarded if family ties weren't appropriate."

What he said may not seem very profound. Perhaps not, but it surprised me. I had not known this man long, but I felt I knew his views. He favored balanced budgets, Yale University, low taxes, high profits, the Union League, reduced government spending, and the Republican party; the code of a typical successful member of the business community in Philadelphia. It had not occurred to me that he was the kind of person who would bring up the fact that ideas, on final analysis, were of major importance.

I wondered if, perhaps, I had not been misjudging businessmen. Was there a deeper awareness behind their nineteenth-century clichés of conservatism uttered at conventions and public gatherings? I decided to try to find out.

The strange thing was that the more I talked to businessmen and economists and reflected over what they were saying, the more certain I came to be that the businessman really had the broader view. The economist seems to have erected for himself artificial barriers that limit his range—seem always to stop him short of the real answer. Other academic disciplines are depended on to take up where he leaves off. Unfortunately, man's nature does not segment itself in perfect coincidence with these distinctions. Man's money-making interests cannot be isolated, they are too complex. The businessman intuitively understands this, and never pauses to wonder if he is answering in terms of good economic principles. He considers all the factors of which he is aware and forms his thinking from these.

In broadest terms the outline for this book plans to first block in the general posture of the businessman on economic matters, then relate this to a range of what are regarded as immediately compelling problems and finally to the sweeping sea changes that still lie offshore but are somewhat seen and sensed.

Part 1 of this book analyzes why the businessman believes as he does, why he frequently conceals his beliefs behind a dated facade, and where economic events are taking him. It is the thesis of this section that the businessman has come to be freed from the automatic discipline imposed by the "invisible hand" of competition. That his own actions have helped free him is, perhaps, the unkindest cut of all. Yet, by the very nature of the business system in which he believes, he feels that he must go on attempting to escape such discipline.

Because he has believed so long and so hard in a free-market system of economics, self-regulated by competition, the businessman is all the more morbid about eventualities at its demise. In his own mind, he has sought to set prices knowing the market wouldn't let him; he has sought to control markets through growth and merger, knowing there is a point at which inefficiencies creep in and size defeats itself; and he has sought advantage of all sorts knowing that the market rewards only those so deserving.

He finds it difficult to imagine that society will permit him to discipline himself if the marketplace can no longer do the whole job. The businessman is not even sure he would trust himself. So he protests loudly that what has happened hasn't really. Inevitably, however, his actions and his beliefs are adding up to a new kind of system, not too different from the old, but different. In the main, the life-or-death aspects of the old market system are no more. It's still a profit and loss system, but less so. The whole thing now is more transparently a game. He is, without acknowledging it, trying to improvise a hand of accepted procedure to replace the familiar invisible hand of competition.

Of more relevance, perhaps, and of more interest, certainly, to most of us than the businessman's view on broadly theoretical economics are his views on the specific economic issues of our times. In Part 2 his opinions concerning economic growth and those public policies designed to effectuate growth are discussed.

The overriding economic problem facing the American economy in the postwar period, which ended in 1957 or thereabouts, was how to halt creeping inflation. It is not being snide to point out that in the late 1940s and on into the early 1950s there was a reluctance on the part of many to admit this as a problem. By now it should be clear that economic growth is to be the transcendent problem of the current decade. Again there are those who seem purposefully slow to recognize what is taking place.

The business community, not so tardy as some in voicing alarm about creeping inflation, seems slow in responding to the dangers inherent in lagging growth. Perhaps, in part, the businessman's myopia on growth arises out of the fact that the problem of creeping inflation has not yet been solved—except in that it creeps ever so much more slowly when growth lags. Perhaps, it is that the businessman perceives that while most of society demands faster growth it continues to cherish institutions and attitudes that are thoroughly inimical to growth, just as formerly an end to inflation was asked in the face of divergent actions.

Part 2 of the book begins with a discussion of economic growth from the point of view of the business community. Chapters 8 to 11 are subjects in and of themselves, but basically they are all related to the problems involved in stimulating growth with public policy. Centralized planning, monetary policy, fiscal policy, and an "incomes" policy are discussed from the standpoint of the attitude of the businessman and the author's evaluation.

What seems to evolve from the businessman's look at growth is the need for new discipline of some sort to replace the invisible hand. Monetary and fiscal policies are fine, but for too long now increases in demand resulting from these measures have substituted for wage, cost, and price corrections. If the market is not going to assume its former dominance, something must replace it. Many measures are advocated, from devaluation to "guidelines." Again, however, the thinking of the businessman leads to some kind of an improvised hand that would determine appropriate wage, cost, and price relationships and trends.

In the final section of the book those developments which seem massive enough to permanently alter the American business system are discussed. The thinking of the businessman should be quite helpful to our society as it meets these challenges.

When the chapter titled "The Peace Scare" was written, the whole notion seemed rather remote. As this book goes to press, however, there seems more of a tendency to look at what life might be like without the present load of defense spending. Likewise, the chapter concerning "Changes in the World Can Change Us" was drafted before Russia bought wheat from the free world. Possibly, therefore, these problems still offshore will be upon us sooner than expected.

Certainly, automation is here now. What is not perceived, however, is that because of it and other developments capital spending seems to be assuming a smaller role in the economy.

Most serious, perhaps, is the threat that derives from abundance. What seems true is that the American industrial system is able to produce enough for a quite satisfactory living standard without employing all of those in the work force with jobs in the traditional sense. The businessman's spoken response to this development is to pretend it does not exist. He goes on asking for more saving, for more investment in machinery, to make more jobs and produce more. The speciousness of his logic invites other answers. All sorts of plans to give income to those not working are being discussed.

In typical fashion, however, the businessman is behaving more realistically than he is talking. As if in subconscious response, a kind of adjustment is forging itself. By a process described here as "reasonable featherbedding," jobs are being created. The truly challenging task will be for business to go on making jobs where need in the customary sense does not exist; and to make these jobs seem, and actually turn out to be, socially, perhaps even industrially, useful.

part 1

The Improvised Hand

2

The Market System

American businessmen are not all cut from the same mold. Some are hard-nosed competitors of the classic variety. Many are "other-directed, Organization Man" types. Most are somewhere in between. A few, it must be admitted, are Cash McCall-like fast-buck operators.

One thing, however, is common to nearly all of them —common at least to all the non-mavericks. In simplest terms, it is their fervent belief in freedom of enterprise, abhorrence of planning for the whole economy, and certainty that the market system maximizes freedom and obviates the need for overall planning. Needless to say, therefore, faith in the market system lies behind much of business thinking insofar as economics is concerned. If this is kept in mind, it is a lot easier to understand and predict the actions of the businessman.

Frequently, I have made this point to my economist friends. It has never gone down well, especially among the academicians. Most professors of economics feel that while businessmen pay lip service to the market system, their actions reveal a beneath-the-surface bent toward planning. "Business wants to be free to form monopolies and divide markets," I've been told on more than one occasion. "Yet in the long run they must know that these actions will beget controls."

Unquestionably, there are some good reasons for believing this way. Many individual actions of businessmen would seem to belie their expressed faith in a free economic system. Actually, however, businessmen do not see the contradiction that seems so obvious to the professor.

That a kind of contradiction exists I would not deny. I was first confronted by it back in 1953. The occasion was my first speech to a convention of businessmen at a resort hotel in the Pocono Mountain area of Pennsylvania. The industry convening will remain unnamed. Suffice it to say that it is an industry that includes a large number of moderate-sized firms competing vigorously with one another.

My speech was scheduled for 11 A.M. I arrived early to look the place over and get a "feel" of the audience. The president of the association was conducting some business preparatory to introducing the first speaker—I was second. A local reporter drew me to the rear of the room for a short interview. When I returned to my seat the first speaker was in full sail. The program said he was a past president of the association and president of a firm in the industry.

Near-panic seized me as I became aware of what he was saying. He was telling the audience that some renegades within the industry were beginning to trim prices just because demand was slowing a little. Obviously, they should be raising prices, he said.

"I am not naming names. They know who they are. They should know what they're doing to our industry. If they don't, I'll tell them. They are leading us back to cutthroat competition. The only way to insure profits is to stick together, keep prices high, and maybe push them higher."

His manner was hard-boiled. He virtually snarled as he referred to those firms cutting prices, but the audience loved it. They smiled with his barbs, scowled when he did, and applauded him generously at the conclusion of his talk.

My observation of the audience only served to heighten the anxiety which came over me after I managed to repress the feeling of panic. I was to follow this speaker with a talk titled "Free Markets and the Federal Reserve System." It would extol the free competitive market, indicate that the Reserve System's decision to discontinue "pegging" government bonds had helped begin a trend back to market principles, point to the tremendous harm that inflation was accomplishing, and call for cooperation with the Fed in its attack on price rises.

Following the past president's speech there was a ten-minute coffee break. Overheard conversation confirmed my suspicions. They loved his talk and agreed with his sentiments 100 per cent. It was too late for an inexperienced speaker to change his talk. What an ordeal this was going to be.

To my astonishment the audience seemed to like me as

much as the first speaker. They appeared to be listening. It occurred to me that they were only being polite.

Following my talk, however, I was congratulated on all sides. Even the first speaker seemed to like immensely what he heard. Luncheon conversation settled the impression. They liked me and agreed with my sentiments 100 per cent.

Why did the business audience just described applaud two speeches contradictory in nature? No one really knows, but what we do know is that sometimes things that happened long ago are an influence. Sometimes contradictions are inbred. So it may be with businessmen. Once the market system was recognized, as if by magic their fortunes improved, their status was raised. Any wonder then that they should cling to it, resist every attempt to change it—except their own. But the market system, from the first, contained the seeds of its own destruction; in a sense dared its users to break out of this mechanism by which a free society hangs together. This may be clearer if we back up a bit and look at some of the events that happened a long time ago and some of the contradictions they bred.

*   *   *

Time was when there were no businessmen. Even after they came into being there was a long period before they acquired much status or real influence over the main course of events. What we have come to understand is that, of all things, a book—by Adam Smith, a Scottish professor of moral philosophy—helped considerably to elevate them to their present high station.

In the second half of the eighteenth century Smith saw a

world still governed by a feudal aristocracy—a world in which some were born rich, some were born poor, and each group stayed that way for life.

Smith also saw the nation-states pursuing mercantilist policies. Governments sought to acquire and retain gold through the imposition of tariffs, quotas, and numerous other regulations.

Smith felt strongly that the surviving feudal and mercantilist institutions and their elaborate apparatus of controls were stifling the emergence of a new and better system. He looked to the new breed of manufacturers and merchants, already challenging the old order, as the activists to bring about beneficial change. His book *The Wealth of Nations,* published in 1776, provided these new forces with their marching song.

The doctrine of Adam Smith revolutionized European society. What he wrote was not a description of the way any economy was operating. What he wrote he believed to be some basic, or—he would have said—natural, laws of economics. Most of what he wrote was not new. But the way he wrote it—tying it together into a complete package describing a natural order of things—almost gave it the status of theology.

Essentially Smith told us that man works best in his own self-interest; therefore he should be permitted to do just that. Out of each of us doing what is best for us individually, common good will flow. In *The Wealth of Nations* he says the businessman is ". . . led by an *invisible hand* to promote an end which was no part of his intention. . . . By pursuing his own interest he frequently promotes that of the society more effectually than when he really intends to promote it. I have never known much good done by those who affected to trade for the public good."

Efficient firms and individuals will prosper, and the inefficient will fail. Interference on the part of the government will only impede these inexorable natural laws. Hands off business was the admonition he gave government. Let businessmen out of their feudal straitjackets, he told the landed aristocracy.

More particularly, the writing of Smith provided the theoretical basis for our price or market system of economics. Price, he said, acts as an adjuster between demand and supply. When supply of a commodity is low and demand for it is large its price will rise. The higher price will act in two ways to adjust demand and supply, Smith theorized.

It will reduce demand, because at the higher price fewer people will want the commodity. In addition, the higher price will induce a somewhat larger supply. Firms will be inclined to expand production because of the larger demand that the high price mirrors. Of course, the opposite reactions are expected when supply is large relative to demand.

Following through with this logic, he said that price —frequently called the price mechanism or market mechanism—allocates resources, meaning that ultimately the relative change in prices determines how much money, land, materials, and labor are devoted to the production of the various goods and services.

Industries in which prices, profits, and wages are rising tend to attract more and better managers and workers, more investment money. They usually build more new plants and buy more machinery and equipment. In other words, resources are attracted by rising prices. It follows that resources move away—relatively at least—where prices are falling.

Smith reasoned that, if let alone, economic activity would be self-equilibrating—activity would by its nature tend toward full employment of all resources. The feeling being, in simplest terms, that when activity sagged, prices and wages would fall and find added demand at the new lower level.

Smith reached similarly happy conclusions about the international economy. Again, if let alone, equilibrium at full employment of resources for all nations would be the natural state of affairs. Nations would tend to emphasize the production of things in which they had comparative advantages. Nations losing wealth would tend to tighten their belts, lower prices, and reverse the unfavorable tide.

The new doctrine was particularly appropriate to the new American society. Political and economic systems in various combinations can be foisted onto a people and they will work after a fashion. But the people of each nation have a somewhat different character. Quite likely, therefore, there is a different political, economic system most suitable for each.

The United States is the only great nation in history that grew up as a business society. Everywhere else the new business breed had to fight the older institutions. But America grew up after Adam Smith had written *The Wealth of Nations*. His philosophy is bred into Americans in a way that is matched nowhere else in the world.

The market system as enunciated by Smith intermeshed harmoniously with the republican form of government that was evolving here. Most important, the market system fit the temper and character of the American people. Remember that these were people who, for the most part, fled from an established order. They sought the adventure, romance, and risk that was a part of the new land. They were religious, but not in the sense of following the precepts of established religions. They had their own religion drawn from their own interpretation of the Bible, and from a feeling that there was some kind of God-made natural law that they understood.

The natural laws of economics as outlined by Smith seemed cut from the same fabric. In effect he gave them an economic system with all the adventure, romance, and risk that they wanted. Even more, he gave them a "religious" economic system—their kind of religion at that.

Very probably, had Smith not written his book and had recognition of the market system been delayed, the United States would still have grown to be a great power. But the guess here is strong that it wouldn't have come so fast, the division of wealth—never perfectly equitable—would not have been so fair, and most certainly everyone would not have felt so good about it all.

Thus, from the beginning the business community accepted the preachments of Smith. Businessmen were delighted to have practical business maxims elevated to the status of a natural law.

Not unnaturally, however, businessmen began immediately to operate individually in an effort to thwart the natural law. They acted this way not with evil intent, not because they didn't believe in the market system; they were merely acting in their own self-interest, as was each of their counterparts. The invisible hand of competition relieved any anxieties that might have beset them over the consequences of their actions. The public good would be served.

And so from the first, businessmen could be called schizophrenic in their attitude toward the price system. Instinctively, they wanted to control the market, not have it control them. They recognized, however, that it was the supremacy of the market that enabled them to act as they did. If the market didn't control them something else would—the government. As a result businessmen as a group deplore rising prices. On the other hand, each businessman wants the goods or service he produces or sells to rise in price.

Unfortunately, candid talk on the matter of market power is inhibited by the fact that some consider it a moral issue. It is not. Every businessman seeks control or influence over the price of his product. This desire grows out of the facts of life in the market.

Firms must make a profit or they fail, and none want that. Basically, of course, profitability depends on being able to sell something for more than it costs to make it. This can sound deceptively simple. Just make something people want, figure out your costs, add a margin for profit, and you are in business to stay.

But suppose someone else making the same product finds a way to make it cheaper—maybe by using new processes of some sort. He reduces his price. You have to go along or lose your customers. Result: no more profits, and no more business unless you find a way to operate profitably at the new lower price the market demands.

Or suppose a new product that to some extent can be substituted for yours comes onto the market. Customers may still prefer your product, but not at the old price. Your price goes down to the level the market dictates and your profit falls or disappears.

Maybe you suddenly have to pay more in wages or for

materials, but market forces hold the price of your product where it was. Again, unless you can adjust, you are out of business.

Every corporation owner or manager must do everything possible to prevent eventualities such as these. The market system tells him he should, dares him to try. From the beginning, businesses have tried to escape from the whim of the marketplace. They have sought to control the market, and not have it control them.

But how do you control a market? You can't make people buy what they don't want. You can't fix a price for your product when someone else can sell the same item for less; when a foreign producer can invade your market.

Central to their efforts has been price. In a market system, price is a key to success. Through a variety of means, firms have sought to control the price at which they sell. To some considerable degree many of them have been successful. How they have achieved the power to price is a complex story which can be told only in abbreviated fashion here.

Tariff protection long has been sought in an effort to shield domestic prices. For a long time tariff walls were reconciled with free-market principles under the "infant-industry" theory. The idea being that firms needed protection from foreign competition until they "grew up" to competitive status. Undeniably, however, tariffs have tended to last into industry maturity. Of course, the essential idea of a tariff is to permit an industry to sell its product at a higher price in the domestic market than would be possible if foreign producers didn't have to pay a tariff before selling here.

The very basic idea of product identification is an early step in an attempt to influence price. The next step is to make a product a little better or, in any event, obviously different in some way from its direct competitors. Then exploit the differences in advertising. Advertising also seeks to create a real need for your particular product so that demand for it will exist independently of demand for the general commodity category in which it fits. Manufactured products intended for personal consumption are always distinguishable from their competitors. For example, white paint looks like white paint, but manufacturers of white paint do not put out the same product. It is packaged, advertised, and sold in a different way—it may even contain somewhat different ingredients.

The idea, of course, is that as long as your product is not the same as your competitors' its price can move independently of competitor prices. Ford, Chevrolet, Rambler, and Lark compete for buyers in roughly the same income range. No two of these makes are identical in any way, including price. To some extent at least, each has achieved independence in pricing by differentiating its product, but the regulator of competition continues to operate—though at times in peculiar ways—by Adam Smith's standards. (For example, it is not unusual that a firm will raise its previously announced prices to stay competitive with its rival. The point being if the one is going to try to raise its profits by raising prices, the other will have to go along.)

Firms have also gained some control over price by growth and merger. The American business system is a profit and loss system. The profitable firms survive. Consistently profitable firms by the very nature of our system grow to quite large size. Many firms have stimulated their growth through merger and consolidation. Some of these actions were taken in an effort to achieve more market power.

Mammoth firms—those which account for about 10 per cent or more of total sales for their industry—almost always have more influence over price than smaller firms. It is incredible at first glance that few of them admit to this. Their very size and the resultant share of total supply they account for gives them at least some power over price.

Large firms, because they place huge orders, can usually influence the terms on which they buy machinery and other necessary materials. To the extent that they can control these costs they can have more influence on the final price of their product. Also, large firms can advertise more. This can help them shape a market of their own, and give them more price independence.

Large firms always have working for them in the minds of their smaller competitors the fear of "massive retaliation." They do not have to threaten. It just makes sense to assume that a huge firm will probably outlast a smaller one in a game of price-cutting. It can absorb losses that would consume the entire capital of a smaller rival. Moment by moment the big company can outbid, outspend, or outlose the small one; and from a series of such momentary advantages it derives an advantage in gaining its large aggregative results. Frequently, therefore, smaller-firm price policy is aimed at not ruffling the feathers of the industry giant or giants.

Most of the time, following the price policy of the giants is not something smaller producers dislike. Big and small firms want control over price. To most small firms, control over price by "big brother" is preferable to having it fluctuate according to the whims of the marketplace. It is not being cynical—merely honest—to observe that the businessman wants freely fluctuating prices for products other than the one he manufactures or sells.

In some industries more influence over price has been achieved than in others. Invariably, those industries with most influence over price are dominated by a few huge, powerful firms. As a result, industries react in different ways to changes in demand. Automobile makers, for example, were able to raise the price of their products in the face of a huge decline in demand from 1955 through 1958.

Despite all of this, businessmen are sure that through their actions they haven't conquered the market. Yes, they will admit that there are those among them who have acquired sufficient power over the market to establish prices within certain limits. But none has enough power to insure income or profits. They say the market has successfully defied them. On the other hand, their actions inhibit or ameliorate market forces, and, they say, other forces (to be discussed in the next chapter) have moved in such a way as to almost sterilize the functioning of the market mechanism. They see themselves as victims of these forces, now operating without gyroscope or compass except as they provide for themselves—uncertain as to just what is keeping the system going except their faith.

3

Maybe It Just Changed Itself

As indicated in the preceding chapter, precious few businessmen believe that through their actions they have really gained control over the market. Obviously they acknowledge that in some industries concentration is such that only a few firms remain to directly compete with each other. But this kind of competition is usually extremely intense. If it does not result in cutthroat price competition that brings with it a mass of dead corporate bodies, still it does eliminate inefficiency through merger or gradual disintegration.

Competition does not exist only between firms in the same industry. There is competition within different units of the same firm. For example, quite likely the Chevrolet Impala (General Motors) had as much to do with the tremendous decline in sales of Buicks (General Motors) in the late 1950s as the Thunderbird (Ford).

More important, however, there is competition between products. Trucks compete with railroads, backyard swimming pools with automobiles, television sets with motion picture attendance, aluminum with steel, margarine with butter, etc.

Finally, there is competition with foreign producers. German Volkswagens, British bikes, and Japanese radios and sports equipment seen everywhere in the United States remind us how keen this rivalry can be.

For very real reasons, then, it is impossible to convince businessmen that competition no longer exists, or that he or his fellows control markets. One reason why he mistrusts most professors of economics is that so many academicians say that markets are controlled. Business considers this view highly naïve. Still, it is part of his mixed makeup that the businessman regards as equally naïve those economists who believe that market discipline is directing the economy.

His reasons for doubting the ultimate supremacy of the market in the present context are somewhat involved. At the outset it might be helpful to list them under three main headings.

First, the businessman believes that the price of labor has been removed from market control. Second, he feels that government policy by enlarging demand in downturns works to inhibit corrections necessary to the working of a market system. And finally, most embarrassingly he sees himself as a manager acting at times inconsistently with what he deems to be the appropriate move for the entrepreneur in a market system.

The market system of Adam Smith envisaged a society in which most of the work was accomplished in small, owner-operated shops, stores, and farms. Until the middle of the nineteenth century the United States was pretty largely a community of self-employed. Since that time a great change has been taking place. We have turned into a community of employees.

It is to be expected that a community of free employees would develop patterns of living different from a self-employed community. Naturally, too, distinctive theories about what makes an economy work and how production and employment can best be stimulated are to be expected.

For some time, accepted theory had it that wages as well as prices should be determined entirely by free-market forces. The notion was that when supply was large relative to demand—more workers than jobs—wages would fall. All would then find work at the new lower wage level. When jobs were plentiful relative to workers, wages would rise. Where wages were highest relatively, labor would be attracted.

Some would say that the theory was never really tested—that almost from the beginning rigidities were built into the wage structure. These rigidities prevented wages from moving fluidly to correct imbalances in the demand for and supply of workers.

In any event, workers do not consider this method of adjustment satisfactory. They reason that when wages are cut this action reduces income, thus spending, and further aggravates the unemployment problem it is supposed to solve. In addition, a decline in wages sets off adverse psychological forces. Spending is postponed in fear of additional cuts.

As a result, workers—like businessmen—have tried mightily to control the price of their services. In the main, American workers have tried to accomplish this through labor organizations. From the start, workers have evinced faith in bargaining procedure to raise income, taking it for granted that a higher price for labor means larger payrolls. Also, they have assumed that larger payrolls can be had by encroaching on profits.

Historically, workers' efforts to organize themselves and gain a measure of control over the price of their labor were hampered by two principal factors: (1) rapid business growth which enabled workers to rise quickly in the economic order and (2) general hostility of the community to labor organizations.

The United States through the first quarter of the twentieth century was still a loose economy—open-ended, optimistic, strategically secure, blessed with an enormous margin for error, able to outrun its mistakes. It was obvious that the market system wasn't functioning perfectly, but in general people were extremely tolerant of the system's inefficiencies and inequities. It was the best economic show in the world and Americans knew it.

Rising living standards along with empty lands to the west and a fluid social structure made the opportunities of the moment seem boundless, while the injustices looked relatively transitory. Within such an environment labor unions had great difficulty making headway.

The Great Depression of the 1930s broke the overwhelming influence of business upon the thinking of the community and removed impediments to the growth of the labor union movement. Today the United States has a large, powerful, and aggressive labor movement. About two-thirds of all manufacturing employees are covered by union contracts. Of all workers outside of agriculture and the professions, about one-third are covered.

Now union-management negotiation is the dominant method of establishing wage rates. Economists debate the effect of unions on wages; they disagree on its magnitude, even its direction. Businessmen have no such doubts. Collective bargaining, they say, affects both the structure and behavior of wages. The structure of wages is likely to reflect the bargaining power of unions rather than the workers' skill. In industries, occupations, or places where unions are strong, wages are higher relative to skill and responsibility. The behavior of wages is less responsive to changes in demand than would be the case if there were no unions. Wage rates are set on a rigidly upward course that is deflected only somewhat by decline in activity. Of course, this is what workers set out to accomplish.

In its accomplishment the supremacy of the market is impaired and business is victimized, say the businessmen. Businessmen frequently say they are in a position where they can't raise prices or foreign competitors will steal their markets, yet with the union asking another wage hike, costs go up.

To the businessman this situation possibly could correct itself if the government would let it. After a speech on "cost-push" inflation to a Philadelphia Chamber of Commerce group in 1958, a businessman came up to me and said:

"What we need is for the government not to take any corrective action during just one recession; that would bring wage rates back under the influence of market forces."

He reasoned that—this was in 1958—government spending was enormous, that in any event private demand would rebound, and unemployment compensation would lift Federal spending some even without overt action; so no great harm would come and a lot of good would be done. Then he added something quite interesting and revealing.

"Of course, I didn't want to suggest this in the question and answer session. They'd think I was some kind of a nut."

Actually, it was relatively recently in the United States that the government felt called on to act directly to avoid economic distress. Of course, the interconnectedness of the political and economic spheres is not peculiar to recent times. The strict separation was always more of a political ideal than a reflection of observable reality; the monetary, tax, and tariff policies of the government had a long time ago, as they have now, a direct bearing on economic life.

But right on through to the early 1900s the notion persisted among most observers that depressions or crises were disasters caused by some unusual occurrence or calamitous chain of events. Even though almost from the beginning the nation was confronted with periodic and serious interruptions in the workings of the economy—in the 1870s and 1890s, for example, the economy suffered through rather long and deep depressions—most observers regarded prosperity as normal, assuming a freely functioning price system. The feeling was that the economy if let alone would right itself.

Naturally, therefore, government efforts to correct depressions were pretty much confined to actions to check monopoly tendencies and to prevent interference with the functioning of the price system.

Even after the idea of a repetitive business cycle was popularized by Wesley Mitchell and others, the call for more or different government action was not popular in this country. Mitchell's book *Business Cycles* showed the cyclical progression from one phase to another as a characteristic feature of the functioning of a free economy. For the most part, however, observers concluded that imperfections in the price system were causing the ups and downs. Still the recipe for government remained the same: hands off the economy except to remove price and wage rigidities.

The deep, prolonged depression beginning in 1929 and the writings of John Maynard Keynes changed all this. Despite the tremendous influence of Keynes, he remains to businessmen a controversial figure. Suffice it to say that Keynes provided an answer to the unemployment problem of the 1930s that probably was more pragmatic than the cure prescribed by the more traditional minded. His theory was not more logical nor more nearly perfect in terms of internal consistency than the traditionalists'. Keynes's theory had profound impact because it offered a course of action which was practicable in the economic world as it existed. Most economists feel that he saved the market system. Many businessmen think he ruined it.

Traditionalists regarded the depression as growing out of rigidities built into the price system. Unemployment, for example, was looked on as a consequence of wages being too high—higher than they would be under thoroughgoing competition among wage earners. The corrective government action implied by this analysis is the customary one of seeking to remove the rigidities. In other words, unemployment could be cured by reductions in wages. The businessman quoted at the Chamber of Commerce still sought this answer. It is interesting, though, that he was embarrassed to express himself this way even before a Chamber of Commerce group. It was because he felt his fellows would think him naïve.

Keynes's analysis tended to accept price and wage rigidities as facts of economic life. He favored attacking the problem of unemployment by manipulating demand rather than by manipulating wages. Lower interest rates to induce investment spending by businessmen and direct government spending to enlarge demand were his prescriptions.

Since the 1930s it has been the general policy of government to accept the persistence of relatively inflexible prices in certain areas of the economy. Reliance has been placed on monetary and fiscal policies to avoid slumps through the maintenance of effective demand. The conclusion has been that if demand is maintained, the price dispersion that is both a consequence and a contributing agent tending to intensify booms and slumps would be important no longer.

Unquestionably, the fact that the Keynesian compensatory spending policies were introduced in the 1930s has had a lot to do with the businessman's slow, painfully reluctant acceptance of these practices. At that time the business community was down, way down. Bankruptcy, failure, and broken dreams were rampant. The community in general and the Roosevelt administration in particular put much of the blame for the devastating depression onto the businessman. The hero of the 1920s had become the villain of the 1930s. He has not recovered completely to this day from the vilification heaped upon him. Psychological scars remain.

At the conclusion of a speech given to the National Convention of Corporate Secretaries in Atlantic City in June, 1962, a member of the audience asked me: "How can you talk in terms of market principles and market forces when for more than 30 years now it has been the policy of government—Democrat and Republican—not to rely on the market system to maintain prosperity?"

The American businessman has always criticized the lessening of reliance on the market that has characterized governmental policy; yet he knows that his own actions are in an effort to prevent the full force of the market from falling on his firm. This, too, is part of the schizophrenia that characterizes the American businessman.

Labor monopolies and government interference in the economy are the culprits businessmen most frequently cite as destroyers of the market system. But subconsciously, at least, business feels that the market system has changed in another way that makes less likely its smooth functioning.

Previously, it was indicated that businessmen do not feel they have power over the market. This seems to be true. But businessmen paradoxically do recognize that in large measure their actions are frequently not in strict conformance with a market economy.

Businessmen believe strongly that for a market system to work, business must try to maximize profits in each market. Yet they realize that for a variety of reasons they are not able to operate in this manner. For one reason, the growth of the diversified large enterprise interferes with this conception.

A firm that produces a variety of products and operates across many markets does not necessarily regard a particular market as a separate unit for determining business policy; therefore it need not attempt to maximize profits in the sale of each of its products. Some products may be classified as moneymaking items, convenience goods, and loss leaders.

The diversification of the large firm minimizes loss in one part by setting it against profit in another. This is a source of strength to the firm. In economic terms, however, such a spreading of risks nullifies, or at least blunts, the effect of changes in prices, costs, and profits as guides to economic activity. Profits from one activity subsidize the continuance of another. Survival of the fittest is abrogated. The selective forces of competition are ineffective.

Of course, management of a huge firm desiring to maximize profits may expand the profitable facilities and eliminate the others. But this doesn't follow automatically. The allocation of costs within a huge, diversified company is usually more the result of a policy decision than a source of one.

Huge size causes other distortions in normal market functioning. An executive sent from a Detroit automobile firm to help run a recently purchased electronic manufacturer said to me: "The more I see of this operation the less reason I see for our buying it. But we bought it and we'll make it go. I really think it was just a matter of our company generating so much in the way of internal funds that we had to do something. Does this make economic sense to you?"

More than the foregoing, however, huge size by necessitating the development of a corporate social conscience strikes at the very foundations of the market system. The modern corporation, if it is really large, simply cannot play the economic game in the traditional manner. It cannot convince itself, even, that an "invisible hand" will cause its selfish actions to be for the common good. It cannot pull out all stops to kill off competition. It cannot even try to make as much profit as it might. Business actions can no longer be predicated on the simple motive of self-interest.

Huge firms respect each other. Competition among them is intense, but there is a feeling of live and let live, cooperation, and recognition of priorities of interest in the hope of recipro-cal recognition. There are even unwritten rules that cause large firms to refuse to try to win away important customers of a large rival.

"The kind of competition we engage in now has us all with ulcers and nervous disorders without declaring total war," an executive of a huge firm based in the Philadelphia area told me.

Huge firms have to pull their punches in dealing with smaller rivals too. Frequently it is wiser to let them live than to compete so viciously as to kill them off and bring on anti-monopoly proceedings of some sort. So the game can never be played on an "all-out" basis.

The modern businessman is keenly aware of this. It trou-bles him more than any of the rest. He can get mad at labor and government for interfering with the market system. He can fight unions and crusade for more conservative govern-ment. But what can he do about himself?

He takes little consolation from those who tell him that the market system is surviving, and that if traditional economic forces no longer play their once dominant role they are still important. Most businessmen will admit that the new system has much to recommend it, but in their heart of hearts they just don't "believe in" the new system. The essence of the market system is that each producer should seek as much profit as is possible. The regulator is competition. If this basis is modified, what is left?

In 1960 I wrote an article looking back at the decade of the fifties. Among many other things it was observed that in the early 1950s our businessmen seemed terribly concerned about socialism. What was happening in Britain and elsewhere heightened anxieties. A continuous stream of articles about "Socialism U.S.A.," or "Creeping Socialism," or "Socialism by Default" poured from the business press. By the end of the decade I reported, "Socialism seems not to be an issue any longer."

This paper was read at a conference in Pittsburgh. An executive of a large steel firm wrote to me and said: "What do the Socialists have to gain anymore? They have won. Most of our big industries have socialized themselves. Ownership of my firm is so widespread as to be properly designated public. Those of us who run the corporation are professional managers, bureaucrats, entrusted to keep it going. Our actions and decisions are based on all kinds of social and economic considerations. If this is capitalism, Norman Thomas should love it."

Not every businessman would go nearly that far, but most of them feel generally as that steel executive expressed himself. Certainly, much has been written and said about the control of firms passing from owner-operators to professional managers. Profits do assume a different role in this new arrangement. Now instead of seeking earnings for the money involved, profit is more a measure of ability—a fair, good, or excellent grade is conferred by the profit ratio. A. A. Berle, Jr., has written about and given a great deal of depth to discussions concerning the changing character of the American economy as it has moved from owner operation to professional management.

Ask a businessman if he wants to go back to market principles—to the system that said simply that the lure of gain, modified only by the regulations that competition brings, should direct our economy—and he will answer resoundingly, yes. Many businessmen will allege that it is labor unions and government philosophy that prohibit the reemergence of a self-directed, self-powered market system. Talk to them long enough, however, and some will come around to a broader viewpoint.

In a sense both labor and government have sought the same goal as the businessman. Labor has sought to insulate its price from the vagaries of market forces. Through union activity and other methods it has been partially successful. Government has attempted to moderate the harsher consequences of market forces on the total economy. Through compensatory tax and spending policies and welfare measures it has been partially successful. Business has sought to control the market rather than be controlled Through tariffs, product identification, growth, and merger it, too, has been partially successful.

One executive told me: "There have been so many changes, maybe you could say the system just changed itself."

All this is not to say that there are not some businessmen who believe it is possible to operate traditionally and that our society should try to permit the economy to run purely on market principles. There are a few, but not nearly so many as might be supposed from the "image" that most people have of the business community. A University of Chicago economist, Milton Friedman, is the best-known among a small group of academicians calling for a return to "pure" market system principles. Presumably he would fragmentize large industry and unions, pull the teeth from monetary and fiscal policies by making them operate automatically, and generally permit competition to regulate the economy. He has a small and inarticulate following among business leaders.

An overwhelming proportion of my economist friends feel that the only reason businessmen want old-style free enterprise is because they know they will never get it. The implication is that businessmen wouldn't want it if they had it or could get it. I don't agree. They would want it if they thought they could get it.

The academic economist and the business leader are quite different psychologically—so different that it is next to impossible for either to put himself in the place of the other. As the economist sees it, business leaders have a more appealing time of it now that the harsh consequences of the market game have been modified. What economists do not fully take into account is that essential to the character of many business leaders is an unswerving confidence that, no matter what the game they would win, they would come out on top. This means that the harshness of the consequences for the loser of the traditional free market game doesn't worry most business leaders; they assume they would be winners. What businessmen think they like about the traditional market game is that they would be permitted to win more, it is fair, and it is not made tedious by a lot of unnecessary rules.

4

An Unwanted Conclusion

The views that I attributed to the businessman in the preceding chapter do not come easy to him. How hard it is for him to admit, even if it is only to himself, that he cannot ever go back to the free-swinging, self-regulated, self-propelled market system that Adam Smith talked about. Businessmen do not ordinarily come to economic conclusions out of abstract reasoning. Economists may sit in their ivory towers and figure things out. Businessmen are more inclined to want to see active evidence. What brought him to this conclusion?

An unwanted conclusion takes a long time forming. When it emerges, as I believe it has, there is a great temptation to look back and say, "This was the turning point.

This was the event that made it clear." But how can it be? All days and all events leave impressions no one of which is completely decisive because each is the unconscious product of that which has gone before. Some are infinitely more important than others. Sometimes it takes many days and many events to form one powerful impression—as with all the days and all the events it has taken to assure the businessman that he hasn't conquered the market. Other times one day and one event can have tremendous impact—as with the shattering suddenness of the stock market crash of 1929.

It has taken many days and many events to bring the businessman to the conclusion that he can't have a self-regulated, self-propelled economy. Some days and events were more important than others, however. Many of the important ones occurred during the years following World War II through to almost the end of the Eisenhower administration. But first let's go back a bit even before the war.

*   *   *

The depression-ridden 1930s were years of great economic and social experiments. It was clear to businessmen that the basic economic game was changed somewhat in that period. Gold coins were removed from circulation and the nation adopted a managed gold bullion standard. Unions emerged enormous and much more powerful. Banks were more regulated and less powerful. Government assumed an entirely new responsibility for adjusting demand to avoid another 1929. Brokers and financiers felt forgotten, old-fashioned. A whole host of welfare measures were permanently added to the expenses of corporations. Businessmen were trying to find their new place in the scheme of things. Then came World

War II. Businessmen forgot for the moment their concern over changes in social order. There was a job to do.

The war effort called for maximum effort from industry and got it. Factories idle or partially idle for nearly a decade were humming again. America recaptured some of the confidence in its business system that had been lost in the depression. In the process of filling war needs huge voids—almost vacuums—were created, and conversely other pockets were filled to overflowing. Producing weapons for war was a tremendous job. It was not possible to add this on to normal civilian goods production. Only a very few nonessential factories, civilian automobiles, houses, refrigerators, radios, washing machines, shoes, nylons, and spareribs, among other things, could be produced for sale.

This was one side of it. On the other side, money and jobs were superabundant. American industry was called on to supply itself and its allies with war goods and food. What a job this was, especially with a labor force thinned by 11 million or so in the Armed Forces. High wages, overtime, and patriotism were used to lure the overaged and the too young into the employment picture.

The situation was loaded with inflationary potential, especially since the war was not paid for from current taxes, and it was decided to check inflation with price controls and rationing. These measures could not cure the inflation virus. They were stopgaps.

Imagine the "setup" facing producers and sellers in 1946. Each spending sector in the economy, except the Federal government, had huge needs left over from the war period. Each spending sector, except the Federal government, had improved considerably its liquid-asset position. And finally each sector, except the Federal government, began the postwar period with a relatively small volume of debt.

But this wasn't all.

The United States emerged from World War II far and away the dominant military and industrial power in the world. Russia had yet to develop the atomic bomb. Productivity of the other industrialized nations of the world was seriously impaired by war devastation. Only the United States seemed capable of producing a surplus for export overseas. Clearly, American businessmen had nothing to fear from foreign producers for a long time to come.

Thus, businessmen found themselves in 1946 faced with a situation where demand backed up by purchasing power far outran potential production, and where price rises couldn't be checked by competition from abroad. Could the American economy, its institutions apparently changed considerably by the 1930s, meet the economic challenges of the aftermath of war?

In view of the above, most liberal thinking and much academic advice suggested a slow, gradual removal of 'the price and wage controls imposed during World War II. Businessmen urged immediate removal. The psychological climate of America in general favored the business view. People were fed up with controls, scarcities, saving, and the drabness of wartime living. They were in the mood for bursting their bounds and cashing their bonds. "We deserve a fling" was the pervasive feeling.

Controls were lifted faster than most economic theoreticians would have liked. Some will always contend that businessmen urged speedy withdrawal so that fast, easy profits could be made. At its best, however, the business view was

that unless the initiative was seized in the favorable psychological climate existing immediately after the war, the United
States would accustom itself to controls and some would
come to be permanent. (Experience in France, England, and
elsewhere tends to indicate that there is some validity in this
reasoning.)

Thus the United States economy found itself soon after the
war without direct control of prices. Obvious inflationary
pressures made some sort of overall restraint or discipline for
the economy clearly desirable—that is, some sort of general
control that would permit maximum freedom for market
forces to reassert themselves and to direct the flow of resources within the economy, but which could be used to curb
excessive overall demand.

A long time ago gold might have been looked to as the
ultimate restraint in a situation of this sort. Assuming a gold
coin standard—meaning gold would circulate as well as act
as a monetary backing, constantly rising prices could be
expected to bring a preference for gold coins as opposed to
other forms of money. (Gold was always worth its weight.)
This would tend to hold in check or to shrink the total
money supply. Gold would be hoarded in private hands and
the printing of moneys based on it restricted. If the money
supply stops growing or even shrinks, overall price rises are
blunted.

Management of the money supply by central bankers has
filled the role gold used to play in just about every modern
industrial nation in the free world. Central bank policy may
be influenced by gold, but there are ways of minimizing this
influence. In the United States gold is used as a cover for the
money supply. The required percentage of gold to be used as

backing for money in 1946 was reduced from 40 per cent to 25 per cent. This provided a huge volume of gold over and above requirements, and assured everyone that inadequate gold would not hamper inflation.

Monetary policy in the United States is administered by the Federal Reserve System. Its job is to manage the money supply in a manner commensurate with full employment, economic growth, and reasonably stable prices. The inflation of the early years following the war tilted prices upward and, the speculative excesses so encouraged, threatened the attainment of the other goals. Unfortunately, monetary policy could not move effectively over these years because the Reserve System was bound by an agreement with the Treasury. The Federal Reserve had promised to support the price of government securities at par to maintain their yield at stated levels. This agreement was established in wartime and was prolonged through the early postwar years out of fear that sharp drops in the prices at which government securities sold would be demoralizing.

The net effect of the agreement was that monetary action to restrain credit expansion could always be nullified by banks selling government securities to the Federal Reserve. Of course, if the Reserve System didn't purchase these securities, their price would fall and yield rise. It was not until 1951 that the Federal Reserve System abrogated this agreement and was able to act effectively to fight inflation.

In the meantime, fiscal policy of the government could have been used to restrain inflation. When the government taxes more than it spends, it exercises a restraining influence on overall demand. The Truman administration attempted to impose this discipline on the economy. But Congress and events were such that in only two years of the first five years after the war was there any surplus.

What this added up to was the fact that the United States moved through the most potentially inflationary situation in its modern history without any consistently applied overall restraint on the economy. Two forces helped prevent expansionary factors from running away with the situation. They were the very vivid memory of the Great Depression, and the self-discipline assumed by the business community.

The Great Depression left an indelible stamp on the mind, the conscience, and the memory of all who lived through it. In fact, the imprint of the depression was so ineradicable that even in the face of sharply rising prices it took some years for public policy to recognize inflation as a challenging problem. "Prices will stop rising soon enough without trying to hold them down" was a feeling many couldn't shake. This feeling, harmful to anti-inflationary government policy, probably prevented many businessmen and consumers from acting in ways that would have aggravated rising prices.

For example, businessmen at first held off from spending all they might have for plant expansion and new equipment in the fear that "normalcy" would soon return, sales would taper off, and new factories and equipment would cost less. Consumer demand for houses, cars, and some other items was inhibited by the feeling that prices would soon come back to their prewar levels. The stock market, always a kind of fever chart that likes to think it stays ahead of business trends, certainly didn't recognize the inflationary potential. It lagged well behind prices and business activity.

Most important to the story here, businessmen exercised a

kind of self-discipline. Not that prices didn't rise—they did. Market forces were too strong to be denied even if the disposition had been such. Surprisingly, however, market forces seemed to be calling for prices to rise faster and further than they did. Upon closer examination it was clear that in some of those industries in which prices were "administered," self-restraint was the order of the day.

For example, the American public was starving for new automobiles. It would be difficult to estimate the schedule of prices that would have equated demand and supply in the years through the late forties and very early fifties.

In any event, automobile makers declined to take full advantage of this situation. List prices were held below what was obviously obtainable, and actually prevailing in the black market. Unquestionably, market forces tended to prevail at the dealer level, but even here the big producers acted to prevent charging as much as the traffic would bear.

Policy decisions in the steel industry in the late forties also served to hold prices beneath the dictates of market forces. Some other large firms in other fields with a degree of price independence refused to permit their prices to skyrocket.

What was unusual about all of this was not that these firms could administer prices in the face of redundant demand; it was that they did. Until then—and to this day—economic textbooks were fond of displaying tables that revealed how certain industries held prices high in the depression years and cut back production and employment. The implication seems to be that prices are always "administered" higher than would eventuate under more freely competitive conditions.

Just as remarkable is the fact that over these years of nearly runaway demand for cars, and lower prices than market conditions called for, tremendous competition within the industry was characteristic. Clearly, it was not a case of mammoth firms dividing up a market, holding prices down to prolong demand, and just enjoying themselves. General Motors, of course, retained its preeminent position throughout. In fact, General Motors, with about 40 to 45 per cent of total sales of American makers in the late 1940s, emerged with 50 to 55 per cent of total sales 10 years later and has held this position. The Chrysler Corporation outdistanced the Ford Motor Company immediately after the war, but soon fell badly behind. Ford emerged with nearly twice the sales volume of Chrysler. Mergers were pretty much necessitated by the weak showing of Kaiser-Fraser, Willys, Packard, Hudson, Nash, and Studebaker corporations.

If the business community talks of free enterprise merely to rationalize its avarice as some allege, would it have acted as it did over this period? In this connection a conversation with a former automobile industry executive and government official is instructive.

"Most Americans are illiterate insofar as the subject of economics is concerned. Fortunately, they like a free enterprise system. Unfortunately, they don't really know what it is. Right after the war the situation was such that demand for our product (automobiles) was tremendous. We could have gotten a much higher price which would have enabled us to bid workers, steel, and other materials away from other producers and satisfy demand sooner.

"But boy, if you think the inflation we had was bad, this would have been worse. Our feeling was that consumers and the government wouldn't stand still for this. Instead of tightening money and operating the budget at a surplus as it should have been anyhow, the administration would have loved to have had an excuse to reimpose price and wage controls. We had to go easy. We felt we had to snub market forces in order to preserve the market. If only the administration had pursued restrictive monetary and fiscal policies, then we could have gone all out without even as much inflation as we had."

From his remarks the ultimate psychology behind business self-restraint over this period may be discerned. Business acted to preserve the market by not taking advantage of it. In so doing, the businessman performed a public service of inestimable value. His direct actions held price rises below their potential. In addition, indirectly the business community by constantly barking at the administration to restrain inflation through overall monetary and fiscal controls helped bring about measures which permitted the emergence of a modern market system.

In 1952, when the American people elected Dwight D. Eisenhower the first Republican president in 20 years, much was expected by the business community. The new officials called themselves a businessman's administration. An economist for one of the automobile companies said to me: "We don't expect to repeal the New Deal, but we do know that by the time this administration leaves office free markets will have returned to the American economic scene."

Businessmen, for the most part, reacted enthusiastically to the preachments of the new team. But they did not clearly understand them. Did the administration really mean old-fashioned free markets? As observed in the preceding chapter businessmen recognize the changes that have come over the American market system. They understand the near permanency of some of these changes.

They wondered, for example, if the administration meant to balance the budget every year. Would it cut spending or raise taxes in the face of a recession? It would have to in order to balance the budget. Businessmen, remember, feel that compensatory spending policies of the government prevent market forces from bringing necessary adjustments in the economy. Would it bring wages back under the direction of market forces by breaking up huge unions? Businessmen are convinced that wage demands of huge unions are nearly impervious to market forces. Would it fragmentize huge firms with power over the market? Businessmen are conscious that many of their actions as managers of massive firms tend to contravene the functioning of a free market. If the administration didn't take these steps, then what did it mean when it talked about a return to free markets?

Fairly soon it came to be clear that the administration did not intend to "rock the boat" too much. What the administration meant by free markets was freer than heretofore. Not so free, however, as to call for the exclusion of compensatory fiscal policies; not so free as to call for the fragmentization of gigantic unions or corporations.

What the administration did was put a great deal of reliance on general monetary controls exercised through the Federal Reserve System. This "freed," to some extent, large corporations from the discipline they had imposed on themselves. Now there was overall restraint. Prices of some goods would rise but others would fall and through monetary magic inflation would be checked. The same magic would moderate recessions since it was commonly assumed that the seeds of recession are sown in the preceding inflationary boom. Curb inflation and you moderate recession.

Corporations were encouraged by more than their own instincts to "take off the wraps" and slug it out. A book by John Kenneth Galbraith, *American Capitalism: The Concept of Countervailing Power,* published in 1952, told them, in simple terms, that power begets countervailing power. In essence he said that huge unions would offset the market power of huge corporations and vice versa. Government could step in and shore up the power of the weak.

Galbraith, a liberal Democrat, serves as another example of the perversity of businessmen. Ostensibly they dislike his ideas intensely. Actually, he has tremendous influence. His books are thoroughly digested by the business community. This one told them what they wanted to hear at just about the time they wanted to hear it. One side of them rejected it because it disavowed Adam Smith's kind of competition, and it came from Galbraith. The other side grabbed it—at arm's length to be sure—because this book told the businessman he could continue doing what comes naturally even if for new reasons.

It was not long before businessmen came to understand that economic life was not to be suddenly made simple once more. Giant corporations learned quickly that they couldn't slug it out, in spite of Galbraith's book. The whole business community learned gradually that inflation was not halted— though slowed—by the magic of monetary policy.

Events in the automobile industry serve to illustrate the point about giant corporations. The Ford automobile was challenging Chevrolet for top sales honors throughout the late 1940s and very early 1950s. Finally, by about 1953 its managers were ready to let it extend itself. In 1954 for the first time in 30 years it took the honors. That year and the next saw a real battle between it and Chevrolet and, just as important, between the other Ford and General Motors lines of cars. By the time the smoke cleared, dead and half-dead corporate bodies were strewn all over. In 1954 these two companies accounted for 82 per cent of total American car sales. Chrysler was groggy on the ropes with 12 per cent and the rest of the makers were merging madly to gain respectable totals.

But it was not only among automobile makers that the carnage took place. Automobile dealers, especially Ford and Chevrolet people, wailed long and loud for congressional action in the wake of this tremendous battle. Their complaint was that the manufacturer was loading them with cars or he wouldn't renew their franchises. Dealers had to sell them at some price or on some terms. This forced them to put pressure on lenders to extend long terms and accept little if any down payments. Lenders and their supervisory agencies did a little howling too. Clearly, businessmen had the evidence to confirm what they strongly suspected but didn't want to believe: that industrial giants can't compete in the classic manner; that self-discipline was to be a permanent part of the American business system.

Just as important was the lesson learned from the behavior of the price level in the middle and late 1950s. In spite of tight money, and even in the midst of recessions, prices rose over this entire period. This was contrary to convention. True enough, price rises slowed to a creep, but the creep seemed inexorable.

In simplest terms, what seemed to have happened was this. Wage rates moved upward nearly oblivious to conditions in the labor market. Corporations pushed the wage increases along in the form of higher prices. When the Federal Reserve System tried to hold the money supply at a level that would prevent prices from creeping upward, unemployment would develop. Wages and prices stayed rigid or even increased a bit during the period of recession because there was a general feeling that government action would not permit the recession to last long or develop much severity. The apparent powerlessness of the Federal government to check creeping inflation pointed up once more the need for self-discipline from within the business community, the impossibility of returning to a self-propelled, self-regulated economic system.

Thus, in a sense, it was the failure of a sympathetic businessman's administration to make the "free market" system work that brought the businessman to his unwanted conclusion. True enough, there are those in the business community who still say that a free-swinging market system would work fine if only unions were destroyed or government kept out of economic affairs. The overwhelming majority of our business leaders, however, recognize that now and for the foreseeable future they have a responsibility to discipline themselves. The luxury of believing in an economic system in which the lure of gain and an invisible hand would steer everyone and the whole economy in the right direction and at the right pace is theirs no longer.

5

The Improvised Hand

David Reisman, in his fine book *The Lonely Crowd,* observes that businessmen behave unrealistically. "When they write articles or make speeches, they like to talk about free enterprise, about tough competition, about risk-taking. These businessmen, of course, are like World War I Legionnaires, talking about the glorious days of yore. Students and many others believe what the businessmen say on these occasions, but they have little opportunity to watch what they do." Reisman goes on to imply, of course, that those who watch the businessman find he acts quite differently from the way he talks.

The Lonely Crowd was written more than a decade ago, but writing today Reisman could very well repeat the preceding paragraph. Is the businessman, then, as is usually inferred, blind to what is going on around him, merely indulging himself in nostalgia, trying to hide the fact that he is going out of style, or trying to slow the forces that are changing his role? Most of all is he just wasting everyone's time by concealing his true identity?

From what has been written so far it should be clear that to some extent it has been ever thus. That is to say that businessmen have always talked one way and acted another. This paradox is built into the market system. What is different now is that businessmen perceive the modifications that have come over the system and privately and reluctantly even acknowledge their permanency. It remains to be explained why they behave this way in the face of admitted evidence, and to assess the impact of this behavior on our society.

In part at least, the businessman is a victim of his own propaganda. He has always been insistent in his public pronouncements on a pure form of free enterprise. "Each man should be free to go wherever his selfish instincts take him. The competition between one man and another will assure society that the necessary tasks will get done in the most efficient manner." To him any compromise with these essentials of the market system has been associated with socialism—even communism.

The sense of what he has said and believed leads him to conclude that socialism is here already. Sometimes he says this. More often, however, he prefers to ignore in his public utterances the conclusion to which his logic has led him. He senses that most Americans like the kind of economic system that prevails. What is to be gained by telling them they like socialism? In any event, he is willing to admit to himself that he has overdrawn the issues for public consumption.

Sometimes, too, he reasons that if he publicly accepts the modifications that have come to the market system, this will soon lead to additional qualifications, and to socialism in fact. If he retreats at all, momentum will be lost.

Much more important, the new system has not been clearly defined for the businessman. This bothers him. In a sense he doesn't understand it. What makes the new system work, gives it motivation, regulates it? No Adam Smith has made it sing for him. He doesn't even know that he will like the sound of the system when it is coherently, logically, and persuasively explained to him. Until he fathoms it he can't believe in it; so he goes on talking as if nothing had changed, or as if he wished that it hadn't changed, or as if it could all change back to the way Adam Smith had it.

To a degree, then, it is possible to theorize that for some time now the businessman has been using his professed belief in the market system to protect himself from an unwanted, undesirable version of what is. Once, in a speech I said, "It is incredible to even think that the market system as envisioned by Adam Smith and the other classical economists could work in a modern setting. In fact, it is altogether likely that it never worked the way it reads. But for a long period Smith's theories made sense, they were close enough to actual events to be believable, they provided a complete rationalization for an economic system that maximized freedom and human dignity, and they furnished an environment within which talent was recognized and rewarded. What we need today is just such an explanation of the American economic system. Until the American businessman gets such a definition he is going to go right on talking 'naïvely' about a nineteenth-century market system."

After the speech a railroad executive from Georgia said to me in essence, "I think you are partially right. If someone would write a new theme song for the American business system, we could stop singing the old tune. But no one will, so we won't. It has all been said. What comes now are just variations on the old theme. Someone may make coherent sense out of the new system, and explain it all lucidly, persuasively, and logically. Like everyone else, however, the businessman responds with his emotions. Someone might convince him logically, but not emotionally. He loves the old song."

Think of all the questions that must be answered once the businessman publicly acknowledges the passing of the old market system. What is the "right" distribution of wealth in this nation? What should be the relation of the wages among automobile workers, coal miners, white-collar employees, lawyers, doctors, and bricklayers? How large should be the profits of a firm? How much more should the president of a company make than his salesmen, factory hands, and others?

If it is no longer enough to say that free competition will result in the best distribution of resources, then the businessman is faced with all kinds of value judgments. Actually, he has been so confronted for some time now, but it has not been made explicit, and public acceptance of the results of his judgments has been enhanced by the notion that it was the market that rendered the verdict. Can the businessman really be expected to renounce that which gives him so much comfort?

There is indeed some reason to wonder if the businessman will ever adopt a new explanation of the American economic system. Not, however, merely because he likes to repeat a familiar refrain, nor merely because the old doctrine answers so many questions. Rather, because by emphasizing market principles he is exerting beneficent influence on the new system that is forming.

In part, this influence arises out of the fact that not only businessmen but nearly all Americans have a certain sentimental attachment to self-reliant free enterprise, to free markets. This means that when the business community criticizes actions that contravene free market principles its voice is heard sympathetically. Of course, this compassion has not prevented many changes from taking place. It has, however, precluded some actions, modified others, and caused a scrutiny of much that otherwise might have come to pass virtually unnoticed.

In particular, the old principles serve as an extremely useful counterbalance to Keynesian economics. Keynesian economics is manipulative. It emphasizes the role of the tinkerer. It suggests that all economic problems can be solved by correct fiscal and/or monetary policies.

Unquestionably, Keynes has made a tremendous contribution to a viable twentieth-century market system. Were it not for his philosophizing, the market system might have been formally buried by now. But in saving the market system, businessmen believe that Keynes sowed the seeds of its possible eventual dissolution. His sophisticated solutions are too easy. They bring about an ebbing of strength, an atrophying of muscle, and a sagging of resistance.

Most of what they say about Keynesian economics seems exaggerated. The business community was deeply embarrassed by its lack of ideas during the Great Depression. Perhaps a magnified resentment of the man who had ideas to spare grows out of this embarrassment. In any event, the businessman's side of the case is not without merit, if frequently overstated.

Although it is not unanimous, a good number of observers of the American economy believe that the depression of the 1930s and slow growth since 1957 derive from the same basic cause: a tendency for increases in productivity to outrun increases in demand. Of course, such a tendency is accompanied by excess capacity in manufacturing, profit problems, unemployment, and lagging income. Assuming a chronic tendency for productivity to transcend demand, the cure prescribed by Keynesians and business leaders provides an interesting example of their divergent views.

Keynesians seem to say treat the symptoms. In the main, they argue for government spending increases to supplement total demand. Spending can be for almost anything from leaf raking to ballistic missiles. The product or the need for it are not the important things. The "compensatory" spending is for the express purpose of absorbing excess capacity and restoring to work the unemployed—removing the symptoms. Just as important, of course, the other symptoms, profits of business and workers' incomes, would be improved too.

Naturally, a hike in spending such as this causes government to operate at a deficit; this is considered highly desirable. After all, to raise tax rates to offset the increase in government spending would snub private spending. This would worsen the basic situation—not to mention the fact that it would be unpopular, thereby jeopardizing the spending increase. Also, Keynesians point out that the deficit would absorb savings idled by the slack demand for credit from slumping businessmen and consumers. Ordinarily an economy growing slowly, or in recession, generates more saving than is demanded. Excess capacity, dim profit potentialities, rising unemployment, and lagging income discourage borrowing.

Businessmen dissent from these measures, calling them narcotics, or palliatives capable of assuaging pain but unable to assure a cure. In fact, they believe the impact of these palliatives may be such as to inhibit lasting healing actions and to produce some unfortunate side effects. What is needed, according to businessmen, is a stream of technological innovations that would keep up consumer demand, and a series of adaptive changes in the output "mix" of industry to conform with changes in consumer demand.

In other words, businessmen feel that total demand can rise rapidly enough if they innovate and produce the things people want. Such actions on their part are the only way to truly restore economic health. The innovations and adaptive changes will come faster, they argue, if government spending doesn't obscure their necessity—if the problem isn't swamped by a flood of dollars and red ink. Businessmen say that they will bring new processes and products to the market faster, and shifts in their product mix will come more smoothly, if some of the normal consequences of the imbalance between production and demand are permitted to obtain—in other words, if they and the economy are permitted to feel a little pain.

In addition to obscuring the problem, businessmen say that redundant government spending sets up other barriers to a real solution. One side effect, they cite, is the relative immobilization of resources. If government spending comes to be counted upon to save the situation, production tends to be "frozen" into rigid patterns. The situation in agriculture exemplifies this tendency. There is a tendency, too, for quality to deteriorate where demand is virtually assured. Some of the incentive for producing a better product is deadened when you know an inferior one will sell. Workers will be inclined to stay on in regions whose market vitality is withering. Prices and wages will lose their sensitivity to the vagaries of demand. Why not just keep raising prices and wages if demand is assured? Responses throughout the economy will move sluggishly.

Businessmen seldom deem it wise to put their point of view forth in the fashion of the preceding paragraphs. It sounds hard, old-fashioned, and depends on a good bit of economic understanding. Instead they are more likely to attack government spending and deficits, particularly the latter. Deficits, they say, are a means of passing on to the next generation the problems of this one. Business publications are fond of announcing to their readers that each baby owes X amount the day he is born. Always it is implied that if the national debt goes much higher, everything will go to pot.

Much of that which is written and said about deficits is bad economics and borders on bold dishonesty. It does serve a purpose, however, in that it appeals to many who would not understand the business case in other terms. Debt and deficits are somehow emotional. People of little economic understanding can feel strongly about them. To some extent, this emotional feeling checks the tendency for many to seek "a free lunch" through Keynesian economics.

Out of this clash between the "narcotic-giving" Keynesians and the "you-gotta-feel-the-pain" businessmen a rather healthy negotiation has arisen. A certain understanding and tolerance of the ideas of the other is developing on each side. Today, Keynesians acknowledge openly that too easy solutions may not be lasting, that "old-fashioned" virtues such as initiative, drive, incentive, motivation, confidence, and the willingness to invest can be important. Businessmen are coming to understand that palliatives are necessary to prevent the sickness from so depressing the economy as to feed on itself and cumulate. Palliatives may provide the economy with time to make more basic adjustments.

Thus, each side has foisted on the other enough of its argument to forge a kind of tacit agreement on the economic principles which govern actions. Something which might be called common consent will flow automatically to business, labor, and government units working within these principles. Actions which contravene these principles must be persuasively explained. The persuasion should precede the action whenever possible. To ignore these simple rules is tantamount to providing an enemy with a damaging weapon.

Government is expected to take action to alleviate recessions, but not such precipitate actions as to sublimate completely what is taking place. The new principles call for an initial attempt to permit the economy to extricate itself. Of course, in the modern context extricating itself means permitting money rates to ease downward—assuming gold considerations permit—and allowing the automatic stabilizers such as progressive income tax rates, unemployment compensation, and farm price supports to raise spending somewhat, reduce the tax take, and throw the budget into deficit. (The necessity for actions in addition to these must be called for manifestly by the situation—or the case for them elaborately made.)

The painstaking manner in which John F. Kennedy in 1962 prepared the nation for his proposal, made to the Congress early in 1963, that tax rates be reduced is an example of the new principles governing Federal compensatory actions. His administration thoroughly "seeded" the idea before it saw the light of day under its auspices. Business and labor support was ardently solicited. The action to be called for demanded such preparation because it went beyond what was expected.

Government also is expected, except in periods of distress, to operate as if rivalry among firms and workers is the invisible hand protecting the public and guiding the economy. In other words, it is expected to permit the market to make as many decisions as possible. In return for this freedom huge firms and powerful unions, with the power to administer prices and wages, it is assumed will follow the direction provided by an improvised hand of accepted procedure. They must behave as they would if competition steered their actions, but in actual fact must never permit themselves to forget their inhibitions and compete in the old-fashioned, all-out way.

Frustrations abound within this vague framework. Leaders are never quite sure how far they may go, but better the vagueness than stifling rules and procedures that might follow if terms were spelled out. Going beyond or contrary to the dictates of the imaginary hand sometimes brings direct retaliation, as in the case of the steel industry in the spring of 1962.

At that time the industry tried to raise its price. Its failure to anticipate the startled reaction to the move is nearly incomprehensible. It was a colossal mistake coming at the time that it did. The industry was operating with a substantial over-hang of excess capacity. Some price weakness was discernible. Foreign producers had made and were making inroads on the American market. In other words, the competitive market signs pointed toward no price increase, maybe a decline.

In addition, a "noninflationary" pact had been reached with the union. The businessman-oriented *Monthly Letter* of the First National City Bank in commenting on this aspect of the move described the event as follows:

"The April 10 price announcement came as a surprise not only to President Kennedy, but to industry and the public at large. The recent steel wage settlement, described by the [then] President as 'noninflationary,' had encouraged the assumption that prices would not be raised.

"It has since been disclosed that neither the President nor the union had any understanding with the steel companies on the matter of prices. Yet the public announcement of a three and one-half per cent general price advance seemed at the time a personal affront to the President, an effort to take unfair advantage of the two and one-half per cent wage settlement negotiated with the help of Labor Secretary Arthur J. Goldberg."

At first businessmen themselves were dismayed by the actions of the industry. Later, sentiment shifted somewhat as President Kennedy and his brother the Attorney General "overkilled" the steel managers. But this did not alter the fact that the steel industry in general, and U.S. Steel in particular, had committed a serious blunder.

The president of a small steel firm in Pennsylvania said to me after the fiasco: "Maybe we didn't want to believe that public opinion meant so much. Maybe we were just blinded by our own feelings about the righteousness of a price increase. There is one thing I am sure of, however, if the public had been prepared for this move and convinced of its soundness, the President or no one else could have rescinded it."

Probably, too, President Kennedy and his Council of Economic Advisers went a bit far with their "guidelines" for wage increases announced in the President's Report of 1962. These were an attempt to spell out what in any event was coming to be accepted—that wage increases on the average must not exceed productivity gains. By making things specific the President made labor and business uneasy, made them fear that the improvised hand was going to turn into a detailed plan. The late President soon sensed this and made few references to specific guides thereafter.

Sometimes retaliation to overstepped bounds is indirect. For example, there is no doubt that unions have considerably less influence today than ten or fifteen years ago. This loss of influence grows out of their flouting of the improvised hand. On more than one occasion they proved they could act contrary to what the consensus believed to be in the public interest, and they seemed to make it stick. However, unions have paid a heavy price in public favor for their contentiousness, and now foreign competition has served to magnify the enormity of some of their actions. As an accepted institution unions are subject to the doctrine of common consent. They continue to behave as outsiders, underdogs who because of their lesser position have public sympathy and understanding no matter what their actions.

To be sure, there are a number of difficulties implicit in the new vague arrangements. Some problems grow out of the much desired vagueness itself. For example, under the new system when is a monopoly a monopoly that should be dissolved or directly controlled by the government in some way? Which mergers are in the public interest, which should not be permitted? If large-firm dominance is accepted in some industries why not in others? How dominant may the large firms become?

These questions are terribly troublesome. Government officials and corporate executives seem to have most difficulty improvising a hand in this area. As yet there is no consensus, no "feel" for what will "go," and for what will be considered contrary to the public interest. There is little wonder. Each industry and firm within it may be subject to slightly different rules with respect to a potential merger, growing out of the degree of concentration already in existence, the economies of scale that might be achieved, the economic health of the industry and firms within it, the impact on employment, and a host of other factors. Perhaps it is part of the new economic environment that business should be kept off-balance in this regard, that government should have the right to "second-guess" mergers.

But difficulties emerging from vagueness do not stop here. A General Motors executive told me a few years ago in essence: "Sometimes we feel as if we are operating with one hand tied behind our back. The crazy thing is that we tied it there ourselves. There have been years among the past few that I have worried about our cars sweeping the decks. I have been afraid they were just too superior to the opposition. Thank goodness Ford's Thunderbird has been such a success. It has helped their whole line. What would happen if we were to get 60 to 65 per cent of the automobile market? We don't know."

A bit of what he said might be discounted as prejudiced. Possibly his view is unique within that organization. But if what he said illustrates the feeling that exists within that great corporation—a feeling of uncertainty, a fear of too much success—this fear would mean that the highest priced and presumably most talented corporate body extant must spend a part of its effort figuring ways to remain in the top position without improving it too much.

To many corporate executives the most vexatious aspect of the improvised hand is the emphasis it forces them to put on public relations activities. In part, their disturbance derives from the fact that they do not understand public relations. The term has unfortunate connotations as far as they are concerned. Many of its practitioners are smooth-talking sharpies of little depth. In other words, businessmen see the seamy side of public relations and regard it as a nuisance.

Fortunately, public relations in the new context has a deeper meaning and purpose. Business cannot expect to gain acceptance for itself in our society if it is not always alert to the public interest and public opinion. It is not enough any longer for executives of large corporations to stay quiet and assume the public believes that market forces are determining policies. The corporation must go out and seek common consent for its actions. The improvised hand can be restrictive or can permit relative freedom of action for the large corporation, depending on public understanding of what the company is doing and why.

Way back in 1928 Walter S. Gifford, then President of the

American Telephone and Telegraph Company, in a speech in Boston said: "We must have a satisfactory financial condition if we are to go forward. In addition to that, we must at all times have public approval because certainly in the United States you can't, no matter what your ability or what your intentions, succeed in the long run without public approval."

What was true for A.T.&T. in 1928 is true for hundreds of corporations today. In 1928 A.T.&T. saw that it had to go out and seek public consent for its actions. In the acquiring of public consent it frequently used market forces as an argument to justify its actions. The position A.T.&T. was in in 1928 is the position many American corporations are in today; they may use market forces as one argument to justify actions, but they can no longer hide behind them. Unfortunately, some corporations don't realize this. Some corporations are still pretending to act as if the market game does in fact exist. Their actions are costing them a lot of money, and perhaps also the economy a lot of growth.

*   *   *

What all of this means, I suppose, is that corporate executives have a purpose in all of this sloganeering and posturing that Reisman and others have noted and ridiculed. Actually, it has served to counteract the too sophisticated solutions offered by the Keynesians. To some extent, however, the businessman has been caught up in his own propaganda and victimized by it. The market game was once a life-and-death struggle of pertinacious rule. Today, transparently, it is not. Where once an obdurate invisible hand of rivalry steered and regulated the economy, today a tractable improvised hand has replaced it. Some corporations by their failure to recognize, or to admit, what is taking place have made themselves a prisoner of the new system. Time was they wheeled and dealed to beat the game that was unbeatable. Now they cringe, awed by their own power. What they do not understand is that they don't have power except as they earn it in the form of consent from the public. Perhaps it will serve to relieve their apprehensions to know that from this new market game as from the old they will get only what they deserve.

6

Implications of the Improvised Hand

Businessmen pay a good bit of attention to economists. The economist's analysis gives a sense of dignity and scientific order to the facts and figures of business activity. Even the special language of the economist is accepted as part of the game; it, after all, adds a kind of eminence to the whole undertaking. Some economists are understandable and entertaining as well as edifying. These usually find special favor. Despite the kinship between them, however, there is a huge difference in the way that the businessman and the economist view the changes that have come over the economic system of the United States.

The present-day economist lives in a world of commodities. It is the behavior of commodities not of men that gets his prime attention. He surrounds himself with statistics on prices, income, interest rates, production, consumption, spending, inventory ratios, etc. From these he builds models, derives rules of behavior and projects trends. Only vaguely does he seem aware that prices, spending, outputs, and the rest are the result of human decisions. He seems to prefer to assume that these decisions are made on a simple, predictable basis.

But the conduct of men is never simple and predictable. This the businessman understands; so he listens to the economist, uses his statistics and analysis for what he thinks they are worth, and acts frequently at variance with the models, rules of behavior, and trends projected for him.

Thus, the economist and businessman approach the economy and the changes that have come to it in a different way. With deft analytic fingers the economist eagerly accepts the challenges that changes bring. He measures their impact on his facts and figures, alters his analysis, and builds new models. He hurries to fit the modifications into a new schematic abstraction of economic order. For the most part he reacts to what is; he doesn't create it.

Businessmen, on the other hand, think first of the human problems that changes might bring. What will be the effect on incentive, discipline, morale, and the general drift of society? They assume basically that men work to satisfy their needs beyond a certain living level for one of two reasons: They are directed to by the state, or they live in an environment which motivates them to extend themselves. Needless to say, the businessman is sure that he does not want to live in a society that must use force to attain its ends, and he is sure that such a society must defeat itself in the long run.

The American business system has prospered because it has fit well with the temperament and character of its people. It has provided an environment within which people would extend themselves. This country was populated by those escaping tyranny, seeking freedom. People of a strict moralistic nature, yet inclined to gamble or they wouldn't have come. People accustomed to hardship, willing to deprive themselves today for the promise of a better tomorrow. People who had flouted laws, but who believed in a right and wrong beyond legalistic conceptions. The philosophy of the free enterprise system harmonized well with these characteristics, and America benefited.

But any system as freewheeling and successful as American capitalism will change, if only because the temper and character of the people who work it change. That has happened here. Americans no longer seek freedom, they feel they have it. They emphasize instead security, which they feel they have not. Americans still talk virtuously and bet freely, but they are not so moralistic nor so inclined to gamble as once was the case. They have become accustomed to affluence, not hardship, and are inclined to borrow from the future rather than to save for it. They have more respect for the law as it is written, attend church regularly, yet are more inclined to violate the "spirit" of the law, and less inclined to live a "Christian" life.

Many of the alterations in the American character are disquieting to the businessman. The businessman does not believe that he has changed this much. He still believes in the old-fashioned virtues—or says he does. Certainly, he thinks the country would be better off if we went back to them. Despite this feeling, he has had to come to some sort of terms with these modifications. For example, he has tried to quench the thirst for security with pensions for overage employees, and goes along, partially at least, with union emphasis on seniority. He doesn't depend so much on tapping personal savings. Now he ensures funds for his corporation through heavy depreciation allowances and reinvestment of earnings before dividends. Always, however, he avers that his heart is with the old principles.

The businessman would probably admit—though reluctantly—that the kind of economic system that prevails in America at the present time harmonizes well with its people. Reisman, in *The Lonely Crowd,* described Americans as now being "other-directed," as contrasted with their "inner-directed" forebears. In simplest terms, to be other-directed suggests that behavior is determined by your assessment of what others will think of you if you act a certain way. Inner-direction assumes a certain inbred feeling for the appropriate moves. In a very real sense our business system could be said to be now subject to other-direction. Large corporations try to guess what others will consider appropriate. The demise of the invisible hand takes away their "innate" feel for what will go.

Even if the kind of economic system that is evolving seems appropriate to its people, the businessman is concerned about its implications. He wonders whether present Americans have the "heart" to keep the American business system at the pinnacle of the world order. He sees much of the romance and glamor taken from the system if his activities are to be circumscribed by an improvised hand of accepted procedure. He feels that caution and slow movement will be the order of the day as more firms come to be aware of and work under the rules of the improvised hand. The safe course seems to be to stay within the existing boundaries of common consent; to stray beyond is to risk reprisal, loss of prestige, maybe even loss of freedom, or so it seems to the businessman.

He has long believed that the business of the United States is business. The very best, most ambitious men in our society enter this endeavor. Business gets those who care about tangible achievements with demonstrable results. If the role of the businessman is limited, qualified, and other-directed, then the most promising men will funnel into other careers: politics, science, the arts, civil service, etc. Clearly, if this is to be the case, American industry will lose its way. If, on the other hand, the businessman ignores the improvised hand, he sees himself cracked down upon, subject to controls in fact rather than inferred.

From this it should be clear why the businessman is bothered by the implications of the improvised hand. By his sights he is on the horns of a dilemma. His choice is between slow or fast death. But is his future under the improvised hand as portentous as he imagines? Has he really no choice, doomed to an unadventurous future no matter what his response? The very essence of the meaning of the improvised hand denies his gloomy conclusions.

Corporations free from the strict direction of the invisible hand can discipline themselves, and they do, but their understandable restraint does not have to confine them narrowly. The sharpest corporate managers seek to enlarge the area of consent within which they operate. In my view, the businessman is clearly right in assuming his ultimate demise as the vital force in our society if he permits himself to be circumscribed by presently construed accepted procedure. However, there is no reason why he should permit himself to be so confined; he may succeed in stretching the bounds of accepted procedure. This does not mean he should act as if the improvised hand doesn't exist. The steel industry tried that in 1962 with disastrous results. It does mean he may seek more flexibility of action for himself in vital areas.

First, the businessman need not be afraid for his corporation to grow proportionately as well as actually. Growth comes naturally to the well-run, efficient firm. Americans like to see superiority rewarded. It is a travesty for such firms to limit their own growth out of fear of punitive action from government. Yet it is probable that firms can get too large for the good of an industry. If each corporation is not trying to grow, talent is wasted or diverted, and growth of the whole economy is stunted.

In this connection, I had an interesting visitor for lunch one day. He was a vice president of a transportation equipment maker. It turned out that he wanted to talk to me about the possibility of his corporation purchasing a bank. He knew nothing about banking or the particular bank his company was considering. He said no one else in his company did either. What they knew was that it would be dangerous to grow larger in their field, they were generating internal funds, and they might as well buy a remote bank as anything else. I talked him out of this idea, but the point is that a lot of corporate talent was being used to search around in unfamiliar fields because management was afraid that to get any larger in its field would bring on the "trustbusters."

Of course, the dominant firm fears that government and the public will view with disfavor any increase in its command over the total output of the industry. What has happened in foreign countries heightens apprehension. In such countries as Germany, France, Italy, Holland, Japan, and even England some huge companies are owned jointly by the government and private stockholders.

Corporations should also feel free to move prices. Businessmen recognize this yet feel powerless to do anything about it. Actions among firms are inhibited in an "other-directed" economy in which each firm tries to guess what others expect it to do, and what they will do to retaliate. The result is a tendency to maintain current prices. Each firm feels that if it cuts prices, others will follow and each will have the same share of the market as before, but be worse off. To raise prices is to risk public censure. Also, if others don't follow, it would involve a huge sales loss.

Unquestionably, for the past twenty years, the ingrained reluctance of business to decrease prices has been far more difficult to overcome than its fear of raising prices. Fear of price war is well grounded. This, however, should not close minds to the potential benefits of cutting prices. Some business minds appeared closed in 1962 when the steel industry argued "that steel demand is not affected by price" and at the same time said, "American steel firms are losing business to foreign firms who are charging less."

Finally, business should feel free to make profits. Psychologist David McClelland recently pointed out in *The Achieving Society* that a man with a high need for achievement likes to know quickly whether he is accomplishing anything and possibly would become frustrated by lack of feedback on how he was doing. Of course, an important measure of the achievement of the businessman is his profit picture. This is like the score to a football team; it tells the corporation whether it won, lost, or tied. As a measure of success, profits play a huge role in a market system. Their existence in some lines and absence in others helps direct the flow of activity.

But if business must be able to feel free to make profits, it should not expect to be insured against losses. Sometimes the businessman behaves as if he thinks profits are something he deserves for operating a business rather than a reward for superior performance. Characteristically profits fluctuate fairly sharply from industry to industry and year to year in a healthy, dynamic economy. To render them otherwise is to detract from a market system.

It is easy to say that business should feel free to grow, to set its prices, and to make large profits. The question is how can business feel free, how can it shuck the mood of paralyzing uncertainty? Too often the businessman is inclined to answer questions such as this by saying the government should do something—let them alone, or maybe crack down on labor unions. But government is just as firmly in the clasp of the improvised hand of its own as business. Business must act in its own behalf, must deserve the freedom it wants and needs. What can business do to secure a more permissive environment?

First, businessmen should stop imitating each other, stop acting in a way that makes each corporation a replica of the other. It is solidly predictable that in television the format of a hit show will be copied many times over. We've run through cycles of variety shows, private eyes, westerns, doctors, etc. So, also, in business there is too much attention paid to what the competition is doing. For example, the Ford

Thunderbird achieved tremendous success shortly after the introduction of its four-seat model in 1958. Since that time every other maker has copied it.

Competition throughout industry has turned defensive in nature. How can the individual corporation have much volition in setting its prices when everything is about the same? The amount of choice among products of one type is decreasing. Nearly identical products must be sold at nearly identical prices. Each firm seems to ape its competitors, seems like its competitors, seems overworried about its competitors, and most important, knows too much about its competitors.

The businessman today knows his competitors' market, their rate of expansion, their inventory policy, what they are developing in the way of new products, whether they are diversifying, and their pricing policies. Time was when knowledge of a field was limited; in this environment the enterprising man made an educated guess, forged ahead, and his profits or the lack of them gave him a real measure of his achievement. Now, with every field researched in the same way, each company does what the others do, limiting profits for all of them.

Margaret Mead, the noted anthropologist, has observed: "Today, it has become customary to use the procedures employed by others, to find out facts which will be—or already are—known to others, so as to do exactly what they are doing, hoping only to outguess competitors by a millimeter in a common field."

Behaving in this way, how can businessmen expect the public to countenance high profits? No one corporation appears that much smarter or better than the others. The general public can hardly distinguish among firms working at roughly the same pace, in an almost identical way, in a common field.

In a sense, businessmen by these lemming-like actions tend to nullify one of the advantages of a free enterprise system over a state-directed economy. A free system is supposed to release the imagination of many men in separately-owned companies to find new and better methods of producing new and better products. If, however, everyone copies everyone else, the next step is to assume that the state may as well direct activities. Businessmen are under no compulsion from the improvised hand or anything else to continue the trend to conformity. If they do not free themselves from this counterfeiting, it will be too much to ask the public to release them from the present bounds of accepted procedure as to their size, prices, and profits.

Next, businessmen must come to understand that it would be healthier for a corporation to fragmentize itself when it reaches the point where additional growth is eschewed. The alternatives to self-breakup seem to be eventual monopoly or holding back. Most Americans do not favor monopoly, and wouldn't reconcile themselves to it even though a corporation gained this position through obvious superiority over all competitors. Deliberately retarding corporate growth to keep it in line with the rest of the industry may prevent government action, but seems basically dishonest, and a terrible waste of corporate talent. It is a little like the basketball players who shaved points. They didn't intend to lose, but they didn't do their best.

Fragmentization by the corporation itself rather than by government has many obvious advantages. Certainly, the corporation is in a better position to discern just when it has reached the point where additional growth endangers the existence of competition within the industry, when it is starting to hold back its own growth. The corporation would be more likely to split itself up in a way that would satisfy its stockholders and cause less commotion than if the split-up came at the direction of government. It would be a tremendous demonstration of the sincerity of the businessman's belief in the market system.

To help too large corporations fracture themselves, businessmen might appoint a commission to prevent monopoly. This commission would be nongovernmental, and membership would be a full-time occupation. For the most part, veteran corporate leaders and economists would be chosen for these posts that would preserve the market system. The commission would establish its own rules as it went along, recognizing that each industry is different.

Third, big business should assume all employees as a fixed cost much as does industry in Japan and some of the European countries. All workers would be put on a salary basis and treated the same as office workers. Profits would bear the brunt and reap the reward of vagaries in business activity. Treating all employees as part of the firm rather than keeping a class of them as hired help will improve morale throughout the business system. It would also create a more favorable climate of public opinion toward the businessman.

Actually, there is every good economic reason for business to assume everyone in the labor force as a fixed cost. Precious few businessmen have properly assimilated into their thinking the tremendous institutional change that was formalized in the Maximum Employment Act of 1946—more popularly known as the full employment act. An overwhelming preponderance of the business community, of course, did not agree with this act when it was passed. (That may in part explain the slow assimilation.) Many still hold out against it. No businessman, however, can escape its implications. All should realize how it has changed the cost structure of business.

What this act means, in essence, is that each person in the labor force is to be employed or to receive income while temporarily unemployed. Through taxes business is going to pay labor, working or not. Obviously, then, from the point of view of the economy as a whole, operations are more efficient at full employment because now the rules of the game are such that the laid-off workers who can't find reemployment stay in the overall cost figures. But they make no productive contribution unless working.

*   *   *

Despite the fact that the businessmen may have the best of intentions in making the improvised hand work, I feel that a word of caution is in order. Remember that from the beginning the businessman has behaved schizophrenically. At present, his better self realizes that a wealthy business system depending for guidance upon an improvised hand of accepted procedure must struggle against an inbred tendency to eschew experimentation and radical departure. The development of resistance to new ideas in a society is not necessarily directly proportionate to its well-being, but to some extent, at least, wealth brings caution, deeply rooted habits, and fixed attitudes. An underbrush of customs and precedents could choke off creative minds and new developments.

The American businessman—though he does not give loud

voice to his apprehensions—is probably ahead of the rest of our society in fearing just such eventualities. Nonetheless, remember that it was his "other self" that helped get us to this point. He loved the completely free, self-adjusting, self-regulating market system; yet in large measure he helped defeat it. Now he fears that a rule-ridden society—especially when rules are vague and self-imposed—will lead to more concern about how things are done and less about whether they are accomplished, and will be stifling to the innovator. Yet it is not at all unlikely that he will be the chief rules-writer if given the chance.

Even now events, most of his own making, are leading the businessman toward a system within which competition is being reduced to tedious refinements on the same theme. More and more, firmly established ways of doing things are coming into being. One side of the businessman has always sought protection from the vagaries of competition, change, and challenge. The businessman may truly say that this side of his personality fought so hard because the odds against him were so long. The fact remains that much of the time this side has won. Perhaps the businessman's better self might actually want to sound this warning, but the peculiarities of his schizophrenia won't so permit. Society should be on guard.

It seems always to be his wont to act in ways that attempt to defeat his better purpose. For example, since the businessman has come to acknowledge—to himself at least—his release from the rule of the invisible hand, he has worried over how resources would be properly allocated. Always before he could say that the marketplace was the best and final authority. If now he must simulate or improvise market conditions, this rationale is weakened though not destroyed. To add to his theoretical problems, however, the businessman for his corporation has sought and secured from fiscal authorities and stockholders the ability to generate gigantic sums of money internally.

As is well known, an increasing and preponderant share of the financing of American corporations comes from internally generated funds. This tendency can only aggravate concern over the allocation of resources in an economy operating beyond the self-regulation of the marketplace.

Capital is being immobilized in particular companies instead of channeling into the capital market and being available to firms that could use it more effectively. An undesirable concentration of power in the hands of existing companies and their expansion into other fields in a manner that cannot be justified on grounds of their efficiency relative to existing firms in those fields are inevitable consequences.

In short, we see once again the inbred contradictions of the American businessman. Despite what we—I certainly—would like to believe, he cannot be relied upon solely to regulate himself or to enlarge the self-imposed confines of the improvised hand. The truth of the matter is that the businessman despite his belief in and affection for the market system—improvised or not—will probably always act in some ways to defeat it.

The Businessman Looks at
the Problem of Economic Growth

7

Growth—a Price Must Be Paid

The overriding economic problem facing the American economy in the postwar period, which ended in 1957 or thereabouts, was how to halt creeping inflation. By now it is clear that lagging economic growth is to be the transcendent problem of the current decade. Concern over it helped elect a President. John F. Kennedy put heavy stress on the "failure" of the Eisenhower administration to keep the economy growing at a healthy pace. Economists seem forever to be charting long-term growth trends, extending them out into the future, and telling us that with this assumption we will be here in 1970, with that assumption there.

To all of this, the businessman has seemed to remain somewhat aloof, almost disinterested. Academicians and politicians are dismayed. They can't understand why businessmen, of all people, shouldn't be as interested in growth as they are.

Actually, the businessman is tremendously interested in economic growth. Over the course of the past few years businessmen have come to recognize that this nation's position vis-à-vis the rest of the world has been changing. At the same time they have been faced with problems of excess capacity, lagging sales, a profit squeeze, and union demands for a shorter workweek. It has not escaped businessmen that the change and the problems all emerge in part from the fact that growth of the United States economy has slowed.

But the businessman, the politician, and the economist speak different languages when talking growth. The politician talks in terms of government spending programs, tax cuts, and planned deficits. The economist's approach is somewhat similar, though more methodical, making it smack of planning. Needless to say the businessman is discouraged by all this. As a result he is hesitant to admit that a problem exists. If he does, he fears the solutions offered by the politicians and the economists will be such as to alter our business system in a way that in the long run will stunt growth, curb freedom, and eliminate the fun.

But the facts of the matter concerning growth keep looming before him. A few years ago Premier Nikita Khrushchev drew a new kind of attention from the American businessman when he made some elaborate boasts about beating this nation in the economic race. Even before that, businessmen were aware that Russia was growing industrially more rapidly than the United States. Business apprehension over this had been soothed by a number of rationalizations: (1) statistics from Russia are of questionable validity; (2) while rate of growth was rapid, Russian totals were relatively small; (3) our educational system seemed to insure technological superiority even when crude production totals were challenged.

Recently these rationalizations have seemed to pale. American businessmen began being admitted to Russia in fairly large number in 1958. Groups studying Russian industry generally attested to the vigor and growth of its productive system. Academicians sojourned in Russia too. They came back impressed by its educational system. With each new Russian space achievement, anxiety was intensified. Businessmen and much of the rest of the United States public were impressed and concerned.

Before long, Russian economic growth was placed in a new perspective, but with small consolation to the United States. It became common to observe that the rate of growth of the Russian economy since the war has been exceeded by Germany and Japan and approximated by growth of Western European nations generally. In fact, just about every industrialized nation in the world has grown faster than the United States. In Japan, for example, gross national product has expanded four times faster than in this country.

Many political leaders and economists have pointed to these statistics as evidence that something is wrong with the American business system. Businessmen instinctively defended themselves. Some of what they have said is pretty bad. For example, they alleged that free market principles were more strictly adhered to in European countries. If market forces were similarly freed in this country we could grow just as fast, they implied. At first, this argument seemed effective, but reality soon smothered it. The fact is that government is more deeply involved in the economies of the other industrial nations of the world than in the United States.

Recently, business has adopted an explanation that emphasizes the difference in the overall climate for growth in this country and abroad. It is more convincing. Without being petty, for example, it seems only fair to point out that the rapid Japanese advance started from a level only half that of the late 1930s. In the United States, of course, output in 1946 was higher than before the war. Over the past three decades, as a whole, output has risen by about the same percentage in the two countries. Virtually the same story applies in Europe and Russia as compared with output here. Postwar progress started from a level well below prewar, and over the past three decades as a whole our rate of growth compares quite favorably.

Viewed in this context, the lag in growth here vis-à-vis the rest of the world assumes somewhat different proportions—it seems not so startling, unique, or menacing. There has been a certain inevitability to all that has happened since the war. What seems true is that foreign industrial powers have had a much greater capacity for growth. Their depressed state at the end of World War II provided a most advantageous takeoff point, especially since the American business system was disposed to aid them so generously.

In addition, our preeminent industrial position made likely a certain wastefulness. Why discipline yourself when you don't have to? Immediately following World War II, when many believed it unlikely that European and other countries could ever hope to earn enough dollars to pay for imports from the United States, John Maynard Keynes predicted that high costs and high living here would restore equilibrium in the rest of the world's balance of payments with this country. It took a while, but what Lord Keynes said was bound to come, came.

But businessmen are aware that this notion of inevitability doesn't answer all questions about lagging growth. In this connection they keep at least two facts in mind: (1) no one really knows how much of the rapid expansion abroad is to be ascribed to the low starting point of the postwar recovery, and how much to growth forces of a continuing nature; (2) since 1957 economic growth in this country has not only fallen short of European standards, it has not kept pace with labor-force increases and improvements in efficiency.

These two facts mean that this nation cannot dodge the necessity of trying to bring about a faster rate of economic growth. Businessmen admit this, if quietly. The big question is, how to do it?

This is a particularly vexing problem for American businessmen. Long-run economic growth is something that they have largely taken for granted. It is not something businessmen have worried over, planned for, or even thought about. It has come naturally and abundantly.

For these reasons, inquiries into growth sponsored or undertaken by business groups seem mostly concerned with characteristics. They are static and statistical. They project, from present birth and marriage rates, population totals for 1970, 1975, or 1980. These projections, we are told, indicate that in those years there will be a market for X number of shoes, automobiles, television sets, houses, and T-bone steaks. Gross national product is projected by taking the average increase per year for the past 50, 25, or 10 years and applying it to the future. Similar means are used to project personal income, industrial production, and many other measurements.

The long run, of course, is made up of a series of short runs. Shorter-term growth also is frequently treated statistically. Budget documents of governments are analyzed for clues to next year's spending. Surveys are conducted to find capital spending plans of businessmen, how many houses builders will start, and what consumers are planning in the way of major purchases.

Deeper, sometimes hidden, forces affecting growth have not been so exhaustively investigated. The businessman and his statisticians have measured the footsteps of the giant of economic growth but seldom have looked into his eyes. It has been more or less assumed that growth will naturally evolve out of America's happy combination of abundant raw materials, large and growing population, and capitalistic system. Now, however, the times seem to demand a look into the eyes of the giant. The businessman is coming to understand this.

It is not difficult to find the forces that make for growth in a political dictatorship and socialist economy like Russia's. Growth is planned. Broadly, the government decides how much of total product should go to the armed services, capital equipment, and consumers. More specifically, industrial leaders are told what and how much to produce. Resources are allocated so that, in theory at least, they can accomplish these goals. Workers are told where to work, how much pay they will receive, and what they may buy. To some extent this works, but it is a brown, drab kind of a society that emerges.

Under our political and economic structure, it is much more difficult to find the forces making for growth. Businessmen are far from unique in their inability to understand and explain just how it comes about. At times the economy appears to be liberated from any systematic causation. But mostly there seems a kind of invisible world of cause and effect, mysterious, full of surprises, yet implacable in its course. It is necessary, therefore, to probe beyond the particular scenes and characters for the hidden laws, for the place where the forces take shape, for the rock upon which the economy rests.

The above paragraph may seem to make the American economy sound unnecessarily complicated. For this reason the following more tangible evidence is added.

Not too long ago the volume of investment or business spending was emphasized as a determinant of economic growth. Consumer spending was a function of income; people would spend a predictable portion of their income. The propensity to consume was fixed. Government spending policies were to be determined with these "truths" as a cornerstone. New theories, maxims, and laws were influenced by them. In other words, investment spending was an independent variable; consumer spending was a dependent variable.

But in the postwar period this theory has been modified by events. For example, the boom in consumer spending in 1955, it was said, touched off the boom in investment spending in 1956 and 1957. The sluggishness of consumer spending since then gets primary responsibility for the sluggishness of the economy.

It is now commonly believed that to a large extent the various sectors of our economy are interdependent. Business spending depends on consumer spending and what business thinks the consumer will spend, and on government spending, and on what business thinks government will spend in case of an economic setback.

Consumer spending is influenced by the level of business and government spending. It is also influenced by expectations—expectations concerning future business spending, jobs or the lack thereof, and potential government policies in the event of a business downturn.

Government spending turns on defense needs, welfare benefits, farm prices, the level of unemployment—which, of course, is influenced by business and consumer spending—and how much it is decided to allocate to highways and schools and for other purposes.

Thus, a change in spending in any one of the three big sectors of the economy might be expected to bring about changes in one or both of the other sectors. This is especially true in the business and consumer sectors—the private part of the economy. In these sectors, changes have consequences that should grow naturally out of the free, or relatively free, play of market forces.

Even this much oversimplified view of our economy in operation gives a notion of its vast complexity. A free or relatively free capitalistic economy is many-sided, mixed, and difficult to describe. It is possible to measure, at any given time, how large it is; but how large it should be, or even could be, no one knows. For this reason, exactly how fast this economy should grow or could grow remains a mystery.

Historically, certain guideposts have been used to indicate whether the rate of growth is appropriate. Unemployment and prices are two broad standards most frequently used. When unemployment increases or, if at a high level, decreases only very slowly, it is assumed that growth is too slow.

When prices rise, it is assumed that the economy is running too fast and growth can't be sustained. These guideposts are useful. In themselves, however, they don't say enough.

They are like thermometers for the economy. They tell what the temperature is, from which inferences may be drawn as to what is wrong. But they don't say why it is wrong. Sometimes they are contradictory as to what is wrong. For months in late 1957 and early 1958 prices were rising and unemployment was increasing. The thermometers seemed to be making conflicting statements: (1) the economy was operating at an unsustainably rapid pace; (2) growth was much too slow. Quite obviously, the thermometers were "out of touch." From the analysis in Part 1 of this book it is possible to see how these thermometers "lost touch." Prices and wages can be established by business and labor instead of being rigidly determined by supply and demand. If the traditional thermometers don't tell much about the appropriateness of rates of growth, what does?

The businessman believes it is possible to say that the appropriate growth rate for a society is compatible with the costs that society is willing to bear. Of course, what this means ultimately is that growth comes with costs attached. Some costs are direct, easy to see: for example, the additional amount of capital investment and human training that is required; the shift of emphasis away from declining industries. Other more subtle costs involve the adjustment of social institutions, of patterns of human life and work, that is necessary if the economic growth potential is to be realized.

Possibly some of these costs may loom too large. Suppose additional economic growth can come only at the expense of freedom of action of the person or the firm, or only if people are willing to postpone present consumption to invest in capital good. Modifications of social practices which could make for greater growth may be delayed indefinitely because the change and the cost are not acceptable to those with the power to make them.

Growth may cost particular regions, industries, and occupations relative or even absolute position. For example, Pennsylvania and West Virginia, the coal industry, and the miner have lost relatively and absolutely because of the rapid growth in the use of other fuels. If groups losing ground can successfully stave off the changes through the use of political power, or if equity considerations justify assistance or protection (tariffs, subsidies, price guarantees), costs are not eliminated. Costs to the adversely affected group may be reduced, but those to society as a whole may well be increased.

Subsidies in any form do not lift the real value of the commodity or service produced. The loss remains—though masked—compared with the more advantageous use of resources involved. The shift of resources away from the area needing subsidy is prolonged unless tied in with other policies encouraging mobility. Businessmen, it is often alleged, favor policies that permit suffering in groups adversely affected by the differential impact of economic growth. It might be more accurate to say that businessmen think more emphasis should be paid to assessing the costs attached to alternative policies. A cost of economic growth is the help given to mitigate its impact. Modification in some forms will impede economic growth unnecessarily. Careful attention must be given to intrusions into the marketplace for this purpose.

This attitude regarding the cost of growth may seem just

an argument propounded to fit the prejudices of our business society. But it is extremely relevant to much that has happened in the United States and the rest of the world. For example, in the postwar period Russia has grown rapidly by curbing the freedom and consumption of its people. In effect, Russia made its people invest instead of consuming. Psychologically, an environment of acceptance was created for this policy by instilling in people fear and hatred of the United States. As the postwar period has worn along, the new Russian rulers have had to relax somewhat and give more resources over to consumption at the expense of some growth.

In the advanced countries of Europe resistance to growth-inducing change after the war was broken down by the tremendous destruction wrought during World War II. Physical evidence was everywhere to remind business and labor groups that this was no time to defend outworn privileges, or to secure the maximum immediate gain. Sacrifices were clearly called for, thus more easily rendered. In what other environment could the rapid "Americanization" of European industry and even social ways have taken place?

The United States, on the other hand, was not—and is not now—operating within a psychological climate conducive to the bearing of policies that emphasized growth over other considerations. It was more difficult to convince Americans that the price of growth was worth paying.

In a sense the businessman believes very simply that to grow you have to want to grow. If you want to grow faster you will be willing to do what is necessary to achieve that end. Even assuming this to be true, how do you create an environment within which the richest nation in the world wants growth—that is, really wants growth, and proves it by the actions that it takes? The answer to this question is complicated a great deal by the fact that in the American economic situation, policies designed to induce growth in the short run might inhibit long-run growth and vice versa.

From 1957 on through the early 1960s the American economy has been growing at an inadequate pace. Particularly frustrating to the politician and the economist is the fact that the problem seems such an easy one to solve. Over this entire period the economy could be said to be underweight—operating below capacity with a significant proportion of its factories and machines idle and unemployment high by accepted standards. In other words, a lot of desirable growth could have taken place just by bringing the economy up to capacity output.

Keynesian economics has the ready answer to this kind of situation: add to demand via government spending. Increased government spending in itself would absorb some excess capacity, put some workers back on the job, and even more, the additional income flowing to workers and corporations would result in more spending; hence, the absorption of more capacity and provision of more jobs. Unfortunately, this sounds simpler than it works out to be. The Eisenhower and Kennedy administrations have each padded government spending a good bit, but growth hasn't been fast enough to restore full economic health.

One reason for this arises out of the fact that government spending hasn't had the stimulative effect on private spending that might have been expected. In 1955, $1 billion of government spending was associated with $5.3 billion of private spending. From 1955 through 1962, government spending increased by $42 billion. If the 1955 relationship had held, private spending would have grown by about $181 billion. Instead, private spending increased by just about $114 billion, and $1 billion of government spending was associated with just $3.7 billion of private spending.

The businessman has many explanations for the sluggish response of the economy to the Keynesian prescription. Most popularly he says that government spending, as with any other narcotic, loses some of its effect with too liberal dosage. It does good in the short run, but has a detrimental impact in the long run. There is something to this. It is a useful argument because it is easy to understand, and it makes good common sense.

More sophisticated voices point up the change in the demand mix since the mid 1950s. For example, most of the growth in consumer spending since 1955 has gone for services—the interest and insurance payments, the operation and maintenance required by homes, furniture, cars, and appliances bought in earlier years. These and other services—such as medical care, foreign travel, and private education—have taken 55 cents of every added dollar spent since 1955. In 1955 this spending accounted for just 36 cents of each consumer spending dollar. On the other hand, spending for durable goods—automobiles, appliances, and furniture—took 14 cents of the consumer spending dollar in 1955 and just 6 cents of the additional dollars thereafter.

The shift toward services and away from durables helps explain the unused capacity available in many manufacturing industries, which had prepared themselves to be able to sell goods at a much faster clip than consumers did, in fact, buy. It helps explain also why government spending couldn't be increased enough to bring about full employment.

Increases in government spending brought about rises in consumer income. The pattern of consumer spending was undergoing a tremendous change from what it had been in the mid-1950s. Most of the added income was being spent on services. Less than half as much of it was being used for automobiles, appliances, and furniture. Workers in these hard goods industries were not readily transferable to service-oriented endeavors. Clearly, however, basic forces in the economy were calling for a shift in resources. Perhaps a tremendous flood of dollars and easy credit from the government sector would have brought about full employment of labor and capital. Given the mood of labor and business—each had inflationitis—this could have come about only at the expense of very rapidly rising prices. The price of services in particular would have soared; as it was it rose.

Perhaps most pertinent to the story here, a torrent of dollars to bring about short-run growth and full employment would have inhibited changes needed to encourage long-run growth. The consumer demand pattern of the earlier postwar years was an abnormal one induced by war-created vacuums in consumer goods production. To attempt to "freeze" this pattern of consumption into the economy of the 1960s would have been an enormous mistake, and would have brought about short-run growth at the expense of long-run growth. For long-run growth to be maximized, resources must move in conformance with new demand patterns. On this general belief the businessman and some of the more sophisticated voices agree. To keep the economy fully employed while moving through a transition period of this sort is a monumental task. It is one thing to observe that the demand for cars is down and the demand for education is up. It is quite another thing for an economy to keep running smoothly while these changes take place.

So the businessman feels sure that the past few years of stunted growth have been necessary to restructure the economy, and to set the stage for faster growth ahead. He is conscious, however, that the restructuring has been slow, has come hard. He privately deplores the lack of mobility of resources that in his mind has stretched out the years of transition into a near decade. For a private economy to work efficiently, productive resources must be responsive to changes in desires and needs.

In a modern industrial economy it is too much to expect a smooth rapid shift of resources in and out of areas of greater and lesser demand. But if productive resources prove rigid, growth is slowed unnecessarily. Many businessmen are at a point where they will admit that resource shifts are presently so inhibited as to unnecessarily slow growth.

In large part, they blame the sluggishness of resource shifts on forces other than those over which they have control: for example, unions that force "featherbedding" on producers; unemployed labor tied by skill and location to declining industries; and government spending programs that blur basic changes in the economy. But, to some extent, they admit that the market structure itself has changed in such a way as to impede the smooth flow of resources.

It is not possible to be precise about shifting resources. But it is possible to say that relative changes in prices and profits have a great deal to do with the flow of resources. Theory has it that an increase in demand for a product tends to cause the price of the product to rise. A rising price brings a higher profit. Resources then tend to flow in the direction of rising prices and profits. At present, prices and probably profits, too, are distorted in a way that tends to nullify theory. Large differences in the size of the corporate units characteristic of our various industries, in part, cause this distortion.

When industries characterized by a few large firms suffer declines in demand they do not necessarily reduce prices. In some cases prices have risen in the face of declines in demand.

Industries in which a fairly large number of firms is characteristic seem to have more of a tendency to behave according to theory. Declines in demand seem more apt to bring declines in prices.

What all this means is that our price system does not work in textbook fashion. Price relationships are distorted by the size and power of the various firms within different industries. These price distortions, therefore, could slow growth.

A Philadelphia banker in 1962 said to me in essence: "Much of the overhang of excess plant and equipment that plagues manufacturing is a consequence of defensive investment in industries dominated by a few large firms. Each company invests more and more to make sure that it maintains its share in the face of increased investment by its competitors. The firms are able to do this because big business which dominates American industry finances itself largely from the internal flow of funds—depreciation charges, undistributed profits and the like. This restricts the flow of funds between industries, freezes resources in place, and slows adaptation to new patterns of demand." There is a lot in what he said.

Inflexible wages can also slow resource shifts and slow growth. Theory teaches that when demand for labor in one industry falls, wages respond and help bring changes that must take place. Today strong unions through collective bargaining often prevent wages from responding and growth suffers.

Businessmen point to the case of a worker who has a well-paid job in a declining industry. Consumers are no longer buying as much of the product he makes. But his wages don't reflect this decline in demand. In fact, his wages may continue to rise until he is laid off. Even after he is laid off, wages of those who remain employed may continue to rise. The unemployed worker may be reluctant to take another job in a different industry or area—possibly at lower pay—because he knows the pay he will receive if he can get his old job back. For a long time he may cling to the hope that he will be rehired.

Businessmen contribute to worker immobility through private pension plans. Workers are reluctant to leave even a rather obviously sinking company if it has a good pension system. Thus the stickiness—the drop-resistant qualities—of both prices and wages is a reason for slower resource shift and slower growth.

Quite possibly another huge force slowing an appropriate shift in resources is defense spending. Actually, a good case can be made that the vast load of defense spending this nation has had to carry is responsible for a fundamental imbalance in the economy. Tax dollars remaining for other kinds of government spending have been fewer as a result. For example, spending on highways since 1946 has formed a smaller part of total spending than in the 1920s or the 1930s. Expenditures for sewage systems, water facilities, schools, and police protection would have received more attention had less been spent on defense.

It is unfortunate that tax dollars have not been so available for these housekeeping functions. In an economy such as ours where interdependence of the sectors is of such critical importance, a kind of symmetry is required. Growth in certain sectors quite naturally calls for increases in certain other sectors. And, in fact, if this derived expansion does not develop, an imbalance is created which jeopardizes growth in each of the parts.

Apply this to automobiles. In the postwar period a tremendous rise in the number of automobiles in use has occurred. In addition—and in spite of the compacts—their average size has increased by maybe one-third. This spectacular growth in number and size calls for more service stations, repair shops, parking lots, mechanics, highways, traffic lights, and motorcycle police among other things.

These "derived demands" called forth by more and larger cars have not all been satisfied. Cars have outgrown in number and size some of their ancillary facilities. Grumblings about inadequate parking facilities, bumper-to-bumper traffic, and huge repair bills are heard everywhere.

Automobiles are not the only consumer goods that seem to have outgrown some of their related facilities. Suburbs filled with new houses have sprouted in what were formerly rural and semirural areas. Department stores, banks, supermarkets, and car washes have moved to the suburbs with consumers. But some suburban schools are overcrowded, water supplies inadequate, and sewer pipes nonexistent.

Unsatisfied derived demands are probably, in turn, slowing consumer demand by causing discontent with some things already purchased. The problem has developed out of the extremely rapid growth in purchases of cars, appliances, houses, and some other consumer items in earlier postwar years. A relative slowing in demand for these items would ordinarily permit a "catch-up" in other spending, but defense needs have first call on tax dollars. The slowing in consumer demand since 1957 has not been accompanied by swollen expenditures for public services.

Business influence on this matter has been a complicating factor. The businessman is usually opposed to government spending for anything but defense. He feels that government leaders and the public at large are only too willing to undertake this other spending. Perhaps he is right. At any rate, his consistent opposition to "pump-priming" public works expenditures has rubbed off on the rest of the community. Now there is probably developing a subconscious tendency for government leaders to "pad" defense expenditures, rather than try to "push through" needed public works, when increased spending by the government is permitted by a slump in private spending.

This tendency plus tensions arising out of Russian moves have led to huge defense expenditures in the postwar period —so much so that military techniques seem to have zoomed well ahead of the rest of the economy. Perhaps this is another reason why government expenditures recently have not seemed able to bring a boom in private spending in their wake. Military techniques are simply too far advanced for civilian utilization. There will be a catching up, but meanwhile this is another evidence of a breakdown in the symmetry required in the various sectors of the economy to produce growth.

Over the periods in this nation's history when growth was quite rapid there is evidence that spending in the various sectors was more or less contemporaneous. For example, government built the canals that helped private trade boom in the 1820s and 1830s. Land grants from government fed the railroad's expansion that produced another surge in growth in the latter part of the nineteenth century. Government paved the roads for the automobile in the 1920s and a new wave of growth. And, of course, wartime production paid for by huge government outlays helped propel the economy in the late 1940s and early 1950s.

This evidence does not convince businessmen that government action can stimulate growth. In each case in the past when it worked, government stimulation of growth was incidental to other purposes—winning wars and providing a basic framework of facilities. Business is supicious of government action in addition to what comes naturally. Leave growth entirely up to private enterprise, businessmen say.

The plain fact of the matter is that the businessman does not think there is much sense in all the specifics of the talk about economic growth. He tends to rest his case on the proposition that growth will come to the extent that a society is willing to pay for it. In this connection, as was explained earlier, he means pay in the broadest sense. Thus, he feels that loss of vitality and momentum in the American economy since 1957 comes most simply from a lowered level of motivation.

The businessman is not sure why motivation has deteriorated. To some degree, he thinks it has deteriorated because people—including himself—have stopped believing in the things they once believed in, the things that gave meaning to their efforts. Perhaps they have grown somewhat soft from easy living. Perhaps they have come to the unfortunate conclusion that intense effort is somehow unsophisticated, that dedication is naïve, that ambition is crude and for the Russians, Germans, and Japanese. Or perhaps all the rules and regulations that seem to inevitably come as a society matures have bottled up energies. Too often the businessman sees that the new successful man in America is not, as traditionally, the man who gets things done, rather it is he who has an ingrained knowledge of the rules and accepted practices, and who conducts himself in the appropriate manner.

In the view of the businessman, rapid economic growth will eventuate once more in America, but not because of government spending, tax cuts, or planning. It will come he feels from some inner spark in the private sector of the economy, and it will come because the business community has recaptured the initiative, drive, incentive, motivation, confidence, and willingness to invest that makes our economy go. That is about as specific as he can be.

8

Planning—Inexpedient, Inexact, Inevitable?

If the businessman is not willing to talk the specifics of economic growth, others are. Frequently, this talk leads to a discussion of the efficacy of national planning. Of course, the term "planning" itself is virtually outlawed by the businessman. The idea permeates nonetheless.

Unquestionably, much of the criticism that the businessman heaps on planners is irrational. It is this unreasonable response of the businessman that gets first attention. What prompts it?

It is that planning strikes at the most fundamental tenets of a market system. In the businessman's terms, the interplay of market forces should bring about the proper allocation of resources; so why planning? The freedom inherent in a market system should bring out the best in each individual, maximizing overall growth; so why planning?

Perhaps even more important, the market game is fun for the businessman. Business for American businessmen is not just something from which they make money. It is an end in itself. Sure they buy big cars, houses, boats, and take expensive vacations. But these are just appurtenances. Businessmen love the game of business. This is where they get their real kicks. Planning takes the joy out of their favorite game.

It even takes the pleasure out of profits. Businessmen love profits. Precious few of them with word or deed give observers any reason whatever to question that statement. Yet I am absolutely certain that the overwhelming majority of businessmen would reject out of hand the promise of a sure increase in profits—short-run and long-run—if national planning by the government came with them. To many economists, politicians, and interested parties this is nothing more than another example of the perversity, orneriness, and downright stupidity of the American businessman.

But what must be appreciated is that planning destroys the significance of profits for the businessman. Profit to the businessman is not just money. Of course, he is acquisitive—he is a human being—and this is one reason he loves profits. It isn't his only reason. Businessmen also find in profits a measure of their success, a confirmation of the rightness of their actions, a rationalization for the frightening power they wield. None of these satisfactions could be derived in the same degree if national planning accompanied larger profits.

Could anyone really imagine that a businessman would feel the same thrill in being able to run a company profitably if this came according to a national plan? Would he work so hard to achieve higher profits if the psychic return were pared down by "the plan"? If the thrill would be the same, if the businessman would work as assiduously, then much that Americans have believed since Adam Smith wrote his book has been specious. Is it any wonder that businessmen abhor the thought of national planning, won't even discuss its merit logically?

And this isn't all. Planning by removing from profits the feeling of deservedness destroys a psychological prop for the businessman. Every day he must make decisions. It is taking a risk of being overly dramatic to say that they are akin to the "command decisions" made by certain officers in wartime. That the officers' decisions can mean life or death is easy to ascertain. Books and movies have recorded the agony, the loneliness of the men making these decisions. Of course, decisions of the businessman are not of the same stripe, but they do influence the course of men's lives.

Daily, the businessman makes decisions that eat at his insides. It is within his power to lift a man and his family from a "one of the mob" existence into executive status. This is fine, but how about the ones left back with the mob? How much difference was there between the man who got the promotion and a few of those who didn't? The businessman must decide whether to promote the steady, plodding, dependable long-term employee, or give the job to the more gifted, sought-after newcomer. Should he force the retirement of an over-the-hill vice president who is stifling those under him? Should he bring in the computers as fast as possible with all the disruptions they must bring to the humans previously performing these functions? How tolerant should he be of the employee whose work is suffering because of worry over marital difficulties?

These problems won't go when and if national planning comes. Their solution will still be in the hands of the businessman. What will change is the feeling of justification for his actions that he is able to wring from the profit figures. Some decisions come terribly hard; it is some consolation to feel that on balance you must be making good ones because the company is still operating in the black.

The foregoing does not represent a persuasive argument in opposition to national planning. It was not intended as such. Rather it may provide an explanation for the deep feeling the businessman has about overall planning.

What is this planning that the businessman hates? Obviously, it can take various forms. There are those who say that the United States is already planning, that the Federal government through its tax-and-spend policies and the Federal Reserve System with its money policy are the architects of a national plan. But the merits of this kind of planning, if it is planning—an argument can be made equally persuasively either way—won't be discussed in this chapter. The kind of planning that draws the particular ire of the business community sets targets for the economy and draws up programs to achieve the goals.

Even as to this type of planning it could be said that the United States is partway there. Democrat Presidents seem inclined to set, or permit their Council of Economic Advisers to set, targets. At the outset of his administration, President Kennedy, for example, observed that growth of 4.5 per cent a year would seem appropriate for this country. In 1961 the United States along with the other members of the Organization for Economic Cooperation and Development set up a target growth rate of 4.1 per cent a year for their combined output up to 1970. Despite the establishment of these goals the United States has not formed any sort of central authority to draw up programs to achieve them.

The example of France seems largely responsible for the increased interest at this time in planning. John F. Kennedy in 1962 asked his Council of Economic Advisers to study the causes of France's rapid growth. He suggested that "different economic planning" might be one of the reasons why "we're not going full blast as they [Western European countries] are." Since World War II the French have established a series of four-year plans. Some other European countries seem inclined to experiment with some sort of planning based on the French system.

Needless to say the American businessman is quite unimpressed with what the French have to say about their experiment with planning. He argues that central planning ultimately means the suppression of private enterprise and political freedom.

Actually, French planning does not smack of the rigid direction of the economy by the government that is peculiar to Russia and the other Communist states. In these countries—with the exception of Yugoslavia—government schedules the economy with the detail of a railway timetable. The comparison between French planning and Communist-nation planning makes this argument of the businessman seem weak.

It is significant, however, that planning in France has steadily enlarged its scope. The first French plan was little more than a statistical projection and a pooling of economic intelligence. Now the reach of French planning is more inclusive. The plan schedules the pace of growth in seemingly ever-increasing detail.

If planning were to come to the United States, there is reason to believe that even more detail might be made necessary by the advanced stage of economic development. The United States—to a degree not really approached in France or elsewhere—has risen well beyond the subsistence floor, and is able to produce a surplus of goods and services beyond that which is generally demanded. Thus, the big questions are different from those encountered in other countries. In this country it is not a matter of increasing the production of bare necessities to meet a virtually certain demand. It is more a matter of deciding what people will want over and above basic needs.

This means that planners to be effective would of necessity proceed two steps further than in France so far. First, the planners would find themselves beyond the area of economic direction and into that of social decision. The plan would decide what products "should" be consumed, not guided by fairly well established standard-of-living norms, but instead by judging which satisfactions are worthwhile and which are after all not befitting.

In some degree this kind of decision-making is already taking place in America. Certain corporations are so large and powerful as to have the ability to decide the type, volume, and price of products coming to the marketplace. These corporations are guided by an appraisal of prospective consumer wants, the profit motive, the pace at which the overall economy is moving, and the opinion of the community, including government and labor. The fact of a plan would "merely" formalize the arrangements. "Merely" is the wrong word insofar as the businessman is concerned. Formalizing the impact of the improvised hand of accepted procedure, bringing government, labor, and others in fact into the boardroom, would change in a fundamental way America's economic game.

Now the businessman makes the important economic decisions. He makes them subject to "other-direction," but they are based on his judgment, and ultimately are his responsibility. Decisions based on his lights have a certain toughness—they must make "good business sense"—that might be lacking under other arrangements. The business community itself might change in composition with planning. Certainly, what was said in an earlier chapter about business attracting the very best talent in our society has application. If business ceases to hold sway in its own domain, talent will go elsewhere. Maybe this will be fine for the arts, politics, and teaching, but it won't be good for business. How will it be for America? The answer must be subjective. One thing is known, however: America attained its present preeminence as a business-oriented civilization.

The second step beyond French planning that might be necessary in this country would be "demand planning." Much of the effort of the planners elsewhere is involved with increasing efficiency per worker so as to increase productive capacity and raise standards of living. Increasing efficiency is a wonderful idea everywhere in the world, but it is much less a "wonderful thing" in the United States. Is increasing productive efficiency really the most critical question for planners in a country failing by a good margin to make use of existing facilities? The Russians and French are making great efforts to raise agricultural output per worker. Need it be mentioned that this hardly seems a problem in this country? Industry generally in this country is more concerned with an indication of who is going to buy the products before stepping up production. What this means is that the planners here would inevitably be tempted to try to induce or even force consumption in some way.

There are many means open to planners short of making people buy certain commodities. Perhaps the government would support prices—purchase output not sold in the market at a certain price—as it does now with some farm products. In Russia the government inserts itself between producer and consumer as a purchaser and reseller. Frequently, this works out with the state buying and selling at a quite different schedule of prices to induce or discourage consumption depending on "planned" output for a particular commodity.

All of this seems to mean that eventually prices, production, and consumption would lose contact with economic reality. If more and more countries turned to planning, "bench-mark" prices from market economies would be fewer. No one would really know what things "should" cost. Increased dependence on the plan would eventuate, and quite likely the businessman's claim that central planning ultimately means the suppression of private enterprise and political freedom would, in part, be substantiated. Planners would have to direct in increasing detail.

The American businessman charges that centralized planning ultimately means a lower standard of living.

The spectacular surge in economic growth and standard of life in France would seem to belie that statement. Planning in

France has worked. But there is more to the story. West Germany and Italy grow at an exciting pace without planning. Lots of factors were working in nearly all European countries favoring growth: a low starting level after wartime destruction, Marshall Plan expenditures, the exhilarating impact of Common Market developments, and the breakthrough of the consumer as a source of demand. In addition, a seemingly bottomless supply of labor as emphasis shifted from inefficient industries including agriculture, fiscal discipline made effective after the devaluation of late 1958, and the cold shower of foreign competition as import restrictions were liberalized, all worked in favor of prosperity and growth in France. This does not mean that planning was not important to economic growth in France. It does mean that planning came in consonance with other favorable developments.

Of course, the fact that planning is working well in France—Japan too, for that matter—does not necessarily mean it would work equally well elsewhere. People, customs, problems and, therefore, solutions differ in the various nations of the world. In Japan, for example, business and government have been cooperating for centuries. Even in West Germany, where there is no centralized planning, a close working relationship exists between government and business. Planning may seem an evolutionary consequence as a further stage of man's mastery of his environment in such a nation.

In the United States, the approach is much different from just about any place else. Government and big business regard each other as countervailing forces. Government is suspicious of bigness in business, and business is at war with big government. The United States was the first nation in the world in which corporate monopoly power was assumed bad. In other countries huge corporations with monopoly power usually have to prove evil to be judged so. Official emphasis in this country is on curbing size, forcing competition. United States antitrust laws in fact and intent are unique, although some other countries have copied from us since the war. The very idea of corporations getting together, as under planning, to discuss output and markets would fly in the face of long established tradition here.

Sheer size and the diversity of the American economy would make centralized planning massive and clumsy. It is one thing to centralize the planning function in countries the size of, say, Japan and France; quite another to accomplish the same trick in China and Russia. In size, at least, the United States is more similar to the latter nations.

Some institutional arrangements which ease the planners' path elsewhere do not exist here. For example, the private capital market in France is extremely thin. The largest commercial banks are owned by the government. Savings used for investment are collected by the Ministry of Finance and its ancillary bodies. Thus, the state has tremendous influence on the capital market, and only a very small part of total investment is financed by the direct issue of stocks and bonds at rates determined by market forces.

This means that in France funds can be funneled into endeavors considered to be in conformance with the plan and can be diverted from others. The Ministry of Finance and its satellite bodies can use financial incentives such as premiums, bonuses, and guarantees to "help" funds into agreed-upon projects. Within this environment it is easier to get industry to follow the plan. Without a similar financial institutional background and with a much more numerous and diversified corporate structure, centralized planners in the United States would have a harder time obtaining compliance with the program. If the plan didn't work so smoothly, neither would the economy; and perhaps growth wouldn't come as abundantly as without centralized planning.

On a more theoretical basis, it seems logical that centralized planning would hamper innovation. Under planning arrangements each industry is "organized" and elects a spokesman. By the nature of things, old-line, powerful companies would tend to dominate these councils. Newer, smaller, less powerful voices may hardly be heard. These minority groups are frequently the innovators. Of course, innovators have difficulty under almost any arrangements; however, planning, with its elaborate system of controls over raw materials, finance, and even manpower, would seem likely to more effectively suppress new idea processes and products. If planning tends to perpetuate the existing structure of industry, it is hard to believe that it would raise living standards in the long run as fast as a freer, less centralized economic system.

Despite these many factors which would seem to make centralized planning inappropriate to the American economy, a drift in this direction is not impossible. It has been about seven years since the United States was in a position of full employment and healthy utilization of capacity. It has come to be believed by many—including many businessmen—that the only way to get the United States economy really healthy again involves inflation. Yet competitive pressure from foreign nations and balance-of-payments problems seem to preclude this solution.

The inflation conceded necessary to bring the economy to full employment is not susceptible to traditional treatment. It is cost inflation rather than demand-induced inflation. Essentially it arises because powerful labor unions and huge, dominant corporations tend to exploit their position when the economy is booming. Wage rates are forced up unnaturally and profit margins raised. Prices rise and markets—gold too—are lost to foreign competitors. Of course, this inflation can be halted by traditional means—restrictive monetary and fiscal policies—but cost inflation starts before full employment is reached. Holding it in check, therefore, necessitates snubbing economic advance and maintaining excessive slack.

The temptation to "plan" full employment, growth, and price stability looms more inviting the longer slack persists. Theoretically, at least, planners can program wage and price stability as well as growth and full employment. This may yet prove an alluring prospect to a land whose every tradition seems contrary to that consummation.

Also, Common Market developments and close ties the United States is trying to work out with this union might make a drift toward planning likely. France seems deeply committed toward planning. It is possible that the French will unofficially lead the European community. The whole idea of the community involves coordination of economic policy. Differences in economic approach among the members are likely to diminish as their business systems become integrated. Already other European countries are copying French planning. If the European community continues perking along at full employment and healthy growth, won't the United States find itself isolated as a market economy? How long will we stay unique if growth continues sluggish? The pull to planning could become irresistible.

Even now, participation in the Organization for Economic Cooperation and Development seems to have brought the United States a step closer to planning. At the first meeting of the OECD—almost as if we wanted to prove "one of the boys"—the United States sponsored a specific growth target. Of course, the subsequent adoption of a 50 per cent increase in combined production during the decade 1961-1970 does not commit the United States to a planning operation of its own. It does, however, surround the notion with favorable omens.

In the final analysis what has always been true will continue true. The market system will have to prove its superiority in action. So far it has proved itself in every test. This is not too much consolation—the players have changed. Now, many nations that were successful market economies are borrowing ideas liberally from socialist-oriented countries —socialist countries are adopting many techniques from market-system nations also, but that is another story. Centralized planning—in a sense the antithesis of the market system—is being introduced in consonance with private enterprise. Adam Smith would be horrified; Roger Blough is. So far, however, it is working. Maybe anything would work within the favorable economic climate prevailing. Perhaps soon, the seemingly basic irreconcilability between centralized planning and a market system will show itself. But we had better not count on it or even hope for such an eventuality. Rather, the U.S. would be well advised to give its system a real chance to show its worth.

Planning would come at great cost to the United States. It would involve the eventual overthrow of many of our most sacred institutions. It might even break the spirit of many of our most productive citizens. But planning can come unless we are able to cure what ails us.

9

That Old Black Magic: Monetary Policy

Unplanned, uncontrolled, undirected market economies, especially the United States, have proved that they can grow rapidly, and raise standards of living appreciably. Unfortunately, the growth and rise in living standards tends to come in bursts. The periods between the advances have been anything but satisfactory. Time was when the American society was willing to tolerate the in-between periods. The Great Depression beginning in 1929 stretched endurance beyond the breaking point. Today there is general agreement that the answer to the recessions and depressions that occur is not to let deflation run its course. Even supposing this might eventually work, the human cost is too high, economically undesirable, and politically impractical.

For this reason businessmen—though more inclined than

any other segment of society to sit back and wait for the market system to adjust itself—have had to pick and choose among the various techniques designed to help the economy avert serious recessionary tendencies. For the most part, it is clear that they prefer to rely mostly on monetary policy as administered by the Federal Reserve.

While this choice strikes most as altogether inevitable for the business community, it was not really that easy to come by. After all, monetary policy by the admission of its practitioners is the art of "leaning against the wind," and "withdrawing the punch bowl just when the party is getting good." Monetary policy makers usually imagine themselves unpopular, even indicate that effective policy precludes approbation.

What then accounts for its acceptance within the business community? The answer to this question is nearly as many-sided, perverse, and paradoxical as the businessman himself. A starting point may involve a discussion of the structure of the organization that administers monetary policy.

The Federal Reserve System is usually described in the orthodox textbooks as a quasi-public, quasi-private institution. This is unintentional obfuscation arising out of the tendency of textbook writers to copy from their predecessors. By now it should be clear that the Federal Reserve is a public institution. It is a part of government, however, that may act at variance with a given administration. It exercises this prerogative with full realization that by doing so it may be jeopardizing its own existence.

Of course, in a sense, any government agency at its own jeopardy may behave contrary to the dictates of the administration. The difference is that the Federal Reserve was deliberately structured to enable such action. By design its structure to some considerable extent insulates it from effective political attack.

The Federal Reserve System was created in 1913 by an Act of Congress delegating to it some congressional responsibility for money matters. What Congress gives it can take away, but the nature of the Federal Reserve System raises some inhibitions to capricious action of this sort.

The ruling body is the seven-man Board of Governors in Washington. These men are all appointed by the President and confirmed by the Senate for 14-year terms, no two of which run concurrently. Obviously, the intent of this arrangement is to divorce the Board from the persuasion of any single administration. One of the seven is designated Chairman for a four-year term. The current Chairman was appointed by Harry Truman, reappointed Chairman by Dwight D. Eisenhower, and reappointed Chairman again by John F. Kennedy.

The seven Governors are housed in one of the finest buildings in Washington and serviced by a staff of economists, statisticians, banking specialists, legal minds, and sundry others. No employees of the Federal Reserve come directly under Civil Service. The System is financed from income of the operations of the 12 Federal Reserve Banks and their 24 branches.

The 12 Federal Reserve Banks and their branches are established as private corporations. Their capital stock is owned by the private commercial banks that are members of the System—the amount subscribed to depends on the size of the commercial bank. Each of the Reserve Banks has a nine-man board of directors, a president, first vice president, and other officers. Every year the Banks show a profit on their operations.

Despite these outward appearances, Reserve Banks are anything but privately owned, profit-seeking institutions. These Banks, located in financial centers, are primarily service institutions for clearing checks, issuing cash, and handling Treasury transactions. They make profits almost entirely as a consequence of System activities in the government bond market, all of which are conducted by the New York Bank at the direction of the Federal Open Market Committee. The FOMC is composed of the seven Governors and five of the presidents. They buy and sell government bonds in an effort to influence business activity, and irrespective of profit eventualities. Their profits, which exceed their expense of operations by gigantic sums, are paid to the Treasury.

Their stockholders—the commercial banks that are members—may receive a maximum of 6 per cent on the capital stock they own. The member banks elect six members of the board of directors of the Reserve Bank in their District. Three additional directors are named from residents of the District by the Board of Governors in Washington. One of these three directors is designated chairman. Each Bank's president—he is the executive officer of the Bank—and first vice president are named by the Governors in Washington.

The directors' powers are in no way comparable to those of a private institution. They serve the very important function, however, of bringing to the president of the Bank economic opinion from around his District. Also they may suggest changes in monetary policy to the Governors in Washington through a proposed change in discount rate—the interest charge made against commercial banks seeking to borrow from the Federal Reserve. Frequently too, the directors interpret back to the community the purposes of and rationale for current monetary policy moves. The dialogue between the president of each Reserve Bank and his board of directors has been a vital factor in the acceptance of money policy by the business community.

Important to the story here is the fact that the complicated structure of the Reserve System—certainly not fully explained in these pages—in large measure helps shield it from attack. Its mixed makeup gives it a natural chameleon-like identity that permits the Reserve System when advantageous to emphasize its private or its public characteristics.

In theory, design, and practice the political leadership of this nation has indicated that it expects independent judgment from the Federal Reserve System. Of course, in any fight to the finish over policy the administration could win. But an open break is not something taken lightly by either side. In the event of a difference of opinion with the administration on an issue of great importance to the economy the mutability of the structure of the System would enable it to get a full hearing for its side of the case.

There is no denying that this ability to oppose current administration policy from a position within the government is one reason for the Reserve System's popularity with the businessman. There is no denying that another reason for the esteem of the business community has to do with the essentially orthodox economic viewpoint associated with the Federal Reserve.

It was not always thus. The image of the Federal Reserve System is conveyed largely through its chairman. Marriner

Eccles, chairman in New Deal days, was regarded as a liberal thinker on economic matters. He supplied President Roosevelt with many new ideas in the 1930s and 1940s. He was not popular with the business community. In the 1950s and early 1960s, however, the image of the System has been projected through Chairman William McChesney Martin. The problems faced over this period have been different from those of the 30s and early 40s.

Free markets, tight money, higher interest rates, balance-of-payments discipline, and fear of inflation are all associated with Chairman Martin. Businessmen like the overall sound of the preceding. It suggests to them an appropriately conservative or "bankerish" point of view. Businessmen see in Chairman Martin a man of sound judgment and mature intellect. To them the Federal Reserve and Chairman Martin are a part of government, but above government. "We'd all be a lot better off if the other government agencies were run like the Federal Reserve System."

In addition, the conservative facade the System projects to the businessman is reinforced by the *Federal Reserve Bulletin,* speeches and statements made by luminaries within the System, and acquaintance with Reserve bankers.

Of course, monetary policy is more than an independent Federal Reserve and a conservative image. Monetary policy is open market operations, interest rates, reserve requirements, gold flows, balance of payments, etc. But basic to all, monetary policy involves adjusting the money supply. Just about all economists and businessmen recognize that variations in the supply of money can have an influence on economic activity. Thus there is no question that one of the ways of attacking business fluctuations could be through money policy.

The difference of opinion revolves around how much confidence should be placed in this method. The businessman says, a lot.

In the United States the Federal Reserve System has been entrusted by Congress to regulate the supply and availability of money in such a way as to contribute to the maintenance of full employment, stable prices, and sustainable economic growth. In the discharge of its obligations the Federal Reserve can by its actions make money easy to borrow and thereby cause its circulation to increase faster than it would otherwise, or make money harder to borrow and cause less money to be in use. Theoretically, at least, it should not be too difficult for money managers to determine in which direction they should be moving. When employment is full and prices are rising, a tighter or harder money policy is in order. When unemployment is excessive, and prices stable to falling, easier money is the appropriate policy move.

Money managers are quick to point out that their policies attempt to influence the course of business activity, not control it and that they cannot force an increase in borrowing but merely permit it. These modestly stated powers of monetary managers form a part of what the businessman likes. The Federal Reserve seems never anxious to claim credit for "saving" the economy, content always to give maximum recognition to the market system for righting itself. The businessman thinks it is nice, too, that Reserve moves are within the framework of the market system and do not seem to threaten its existence.

Monetary policy works through the private commercial banks of this country. That makes for no small problem—there are a lot of them, over 13,000. Each of these banks is a private corporation and is motivated as most other private corporations. Bankers, just as other corporate managers, have come to realize and accept the fact that they have some public responsibilities; but they are in business primarily to make profits. In other words, they are swayed by the ordinary impulses of private business rather than by the dictates of public policy. The Reserve System attempts by its policies to harmonize the self-interest of private banks with the public interest of the entire economy.

When the Federal Reserve finds business activity lagging it takes action to permit banks to hold more lendable funds. Usually the Reserve will buy government securities in the market. When the Federal Reserve buys, it adds money to the total supply. The former owners of the securities purchased will place at least a part of the proceeds in commercial banks. Thus banks get new deposits. The only way banks have to make earnings with these deposits is to find customers to borrow. So the Federal Reserve action causes banks in their self-interest to lower interest rates, and seek new business. Within this environment some borrowing and investment takes place that otherwise would not. Businessmen whose profit potentialities were dim at 6 per cent might borrow for expansion at 4 per cent.

In the opposite direction, when the economy is racing too fast and prices are rising, Federal Reserve policy restricts the supply of lendable funds, usually by selling government securities. Since the Reserve System does not have to be concerned about profits it can always sell its securities by pricing them attractively. When it sells, purchasers withdraw deposits from commercial banks and pay the Federal Reserve. This extinguishes some commercial bank funds for lending.

Banks to maintain earnings must charge higher interest rates of would-be borrowers—in effect, ration credit. Business activity is slowed somewhat and stability restored.

Whether monetary policy seeks to slow or speed the flow of credit it works through market forces. The Federal Reserve influences commercial banks in their own interest to do what is best for the whole economy. The appeal to businessmen of such a "painless," noncoercive form of control is irresistible. The business community likes the way the System chooses to operate according to the rules of the "free market." It likes the way the Federal Reserve bobs, weaves, and jabs instead of standing toe to toe and slugging it out; that the preference is for indirect rather than direct means of control.

It must be noted, however, that businessmen have a slight tongue-in-cheek aspect to their admiration and acceptance of monetary policy. For example, I have had numerous close friends within the business community express wonderment that Federal Reserve people and economists "really believe tinkering with interest rates influences business decisions." On the other hand, these businessmen are usually delighted that many do believe this, because "it keeps the government from trying something else." In other words, in their consistent schizophrenic style, businessmen like monetary policy in part because they think it is, after all, rather meaningless.

An honest evaluation of monetary policy could begin by admitting it does not deserve the nearly complete reliance the business community would place upon it, nor the cynicism with which many privately view it. Under certain circumstances monetary policy can be a powerful tool for arresting inflation and inhibiting recessionary tendencies. Perhaps unfortunately, events have conspired in such a way as to minimize the role traditional money policy can play in influencing the course of business activity.

Monetary policy, for maximum utility, assumes a simpler world where prices rise only when demand is excessive, where wages fall in declining industries, where capital and labor are mobile, where gold outflows exert discipline on domestic prices, and where nations all play by the same rules.

That the above "ideal" conditions do not prevail causes orthodox monetary management of the economy to bump up against seemingly irreconcilable conflicts. Monetary practitioners like to say that the goals of full employment, price stability, and economic growth are compatible. They are, theoretically. Actually, however, during the entire postwar period the Reserve System has had to select among these goals. Because powerful unions and corporations have the power to price, and choose to price beyond the level market forces would dictate, "full employment" can't be reached in the American economy without overall price rises. In fact the price indexes usually begin rising a good bit before full employment is a fact.

What happens is that in a period of slack in the economy the Federal Reserve adopts an easy money policy. If recessionary forces are not overly strong, easy money plus automatic stabilizers built into our fiscal system (discussed in the next chapter) moderate the downturn and help business activity to soon resume its upward advance. Before demand gathers enough momentum to fully utilize resources—including labor—wages and prices begin rising.

At this point the Federal Reserve must decide whether to

accept price rises and continue an easy money policy until capacity utilization is reached, or to begin curbing demand with tight money and higher interest rates. Until the latter 1950s and early 1960s it could be argued that the inflation involved was really not that harmful. Other industrialized nations did not have the industrial potential to compete with us at any price. It was easy to accept a little inflation to secure full employment and economic growth.

More recently, however, price rises have come at the expense of increased competition from foreigners, giving rise to the feeling that a little slack in the economy is a cost that must be borne to maintain price stability. To bring the economy to full employment and to permit the price rises that would ensue would be self-defeating. Markets abroad and in this country would be lost to foreign competitors and long-run growth here would be impaired at the expense of temporary full employment.

In vastly oversimplified terms it is possible to say that in early postwar years monetary policy emphasized full employment at the expense of persistently rising prices. Economic growth was not consciously sought as a matter of policy. More recently a changing world has called for a change in policy. Under the new conditions monetary policy has put more emphasis on price stability and economic growth. The feeling is that a moderation in wage and price increases in this country as compared with Europe is needed to restore our competitive advantage and provide the appropriate climate for healthy long-run growth. The policy has succeeded in that costs in the United States have risen more slowly than in the rest of the industrialized world, but at the cost of excessive unemployment.

In earlier postwar years monetary practitioners in this country would have been excused had they forgotten that gold flows could influence their policies. The United States had about 60 per cent of the free world's gold and maybe twice as much as it needed to back its money. Recent substantial gold losses have brought the United States stock down one-third from the level in 1949. The outflow has been so serious as to cause the Federal Reserve to have to add to its goals of full employment, price stability, and economic growth one of protecting the gold supply.

The outflow of gold must be taken seriously. Businessmen take it more seriously than others. Under existing arrangements Federal Reserve ability to manage the supply of money depends on its holding gold certificates on the United States stock in excess of a 25 per cent "cover" needed for its obligations. In other words, the Federal Reserve can only create new credit or money to the extent that it has at least 25 per cent backing in gold.

Of course, there is really nothing inviolate about the 25 per cent. At the end of World War II Congress reduced the percentage needed down from 40 per cent. Most foreign nations have no formal gold cover requirements. Nonetheless, in the absence of a definite action from the Congress the Federal Reserve must act to protect the present money arrangements. How the Federal Reserve has gone about this is influenced by the nature of the forces bringing about the gold loss.

It is traditional that an outflow of gold occurs when a nation's imports of goods and services exceed its exports, and as a result finds itself sending more money to foreigners than it receives from them. In the current situation, the United

States finds itself sending more money overseas than it gets from there, but not because imports exceed exports. This nation has had a rather large export balance over the whole period since the war. This favorable balance has not diminished seriously. The excess of outpayments has occurred largely because of aid, loans, and investments flowing abroad.

In the period 1949 to 1956 the United States' deficit in its balance of payments with foreign countries averaged $1.5 billion a year. This deficit, though substantial, was not considered at all alarming. It was generally agreed that the unfavorable balance merely reflected necessary financial assistance given other countries and military spending abroad. Everyone conceded that monetary reserves of the rest of the world needed restoration. Over this period little gold flowed overseas. Foreign countries were content to store dollars and not bother to convert them to gold.

The Suez crisis in 1957 put the United States payments position in a kind of "artificial" surplus for that year. Blocking of the Suez Canal caused Europe to import from this country in unusual volume to more than counterbalance aid, etc., going abroad. In the years after 1957 the picture darkened considerably.

Overall balance of payments deficits in 1958 and through the early 1960s averaged nearly twice as large as formerly. The primary cause of the outpayments appeared to be the same as formerly. Aid funds and military expenditures were substantial; however, the fact that capital was able to move much more easily and confidently to Europe and Japan for short- and long-term investment seemed to make the situation less amenable to ready solution. In any event, clearly the world saw the United States payments deficit in different light. Whereas before, foreign countries accumulated dollar balances, after 1957 they were more inclined to draw out gold.

What seemed to happen was that the rest of the world suddenly began wondering if the United States could get its house back in order, and was betting modestly that this country had grown so accustomed to high living as to be unable to accept discipline.

Of course, much of the rearrangement of the gold supply of the free world was an altogether inescapable consequence of our own policies. To the extent that gold is some kind of measure of the relative wealth of nations, some shift away from the United States was in order. Policies of this country recognized that the other industrial countries in the world were unduly depressed as compared with us at the end of World War II. We helped them grow fast in the first decade thereafter relative to growth in the United States. In a real sense then, a reapportionment of gold, a measure of comparative wealth among nations, was due. It is now true, however, that the flow of gold away from the United States exceeds that which can be accepted with complacency.

Policy in this country has had to attempt to give confidence to foreign bankers so they would hold dollars and not convert them to gold, and to keep interest rates high enough to keep funds from going overseas to find more profitable yields. The orthodoxy of Chairman Martin of the Reserve System has been, perhaps, the most valuable asset of the United States in giving a feeling of assurance to foreign bankers. Abandonment of a "bills only"[1] policy in the purchasing of government securities by the Federal Reserve and selective purchases throughout the maturity range have been relied upon to raise certain interest rates in this country.

The Reserve System has used higher interest rates to get investors, businesses, and banks to lend their cash here instead of abroad. It has never been possible to go all out with this policy, because higher interest rates, especially for long-term credit, are bad for domestic business. The Federal Reserve has attempted to concentrate the boost in rates onto short-term funds. This is the kind of money that moves most swiftly across international borders. These rates may not have as much influence on domestic business conditions as rates on longer-term issues. The theory is that businessmen are apprehensive about committing themselves to pay high rates for years ahead to put a new plant or other major installation in place, but they don't mind so much in the case of a loan that will be repaid in a few months.

Of course, it is not entirely possible to accomplish what the Reserve sets out to do. After all, the only way to raise rates is to restrict the supply of lendable funds. As clever as you are in doing this, it must sooner or later influence all interest rates. Long rates must move with short rates because lenders or borrowers can switch from one to the other.

Adding everything together, since 1958 the United States economy has been plagued with excessive slack as reflected by

[1] The "bills only" policy was adopted by the Reserve System in the early 1950s as a move in the direction of free markets. It committed the System to deal in Treasury bills when it traded in securities to influence money conditions. A few years of this policy gave rise to a feeling on the part of some that it unnecessarily restricted monetary policy flexibility. It was abandoned when higher short-term rates were in order.

the fact that unemployment has averaged 6 per cent of the labor force, and industrial capacity has been obviously underutilized. Consumer prices have risen quite slowly, mainly in response to pressure from the cost of services; wholesale prices have been steady to falling. Economic growth has been proceeding, but at an unsatisfactory pace by any standard. The United States payments position with the rest of the world has been persistently unbalanced, resulting in a flow of dollars and gold from this country.

Excessive unemployment and slow growth call for easy money. Stable prices would seem to permit easy money. To cure an outflow of gold, tight money is the orthodox prescription.

In actual fact, monetary managers have maintained easier conditions than warranted by the outflow of gold, and tighter money than called for by domestic business developments. In other words, a kind of compromise has evolved. To be sure, some would say that money has been easy enough to promote domestic business, and interest rates have been high enough to restrain the gold outflow. Unquestionably, that sounds better.

What seems true is that monetary policy has not been able to bring full employment and faster growth nor to halt the outflow of gold. On the other hand, the situation would have been worse had it not been for monetary policy. Time has been purchased to redress some balances in our business society. As previously mentioned, Europe's costs and prices have been rising much faster recently. This could mean that the cause of long-run growth in the United States has been served during the stalemate.

Monetary policy can work efficiently and quickly only

when the market system itself is operating according to traditional principles. To the extent that market forces are violated by powerful labor unions, huge corporations, and unorthodox policies in other nations, orthodox monetary policy will be of minimum value. The monetary manager in today's world can be effective only to the extent that his orthodox prescriptions are supplemented by measures that take account of the economic game as it is really played.

10

Fiscal Policy—a Big Unnoticed Change

One winter night in 1962 I talked at a downtown club in Philadelphia to a group of young business executives. My speech rambled over the course of monetary policy in the postwar period. To some extent, of course, I appeared as an advocate and defender of Federal Reserve policy. The audience was interested, attentive, and sympathetic. At its conclusion, I received a number of friendly questions. I sat down to listen to the other speaker of the evening, a quite capable professor from a university in Philadelphia.

The professor's talk was designed as mine, except that he was talking about fiscal policy in the postwar period. His attitude suggested more reliance should have been placed on compensatory tax-and-spend policy. Now, however, it was clear in looking about the room that the audience, while still interested and attentive, was decidedly unsympathetic. When he finished, feeling in the room was confirmed by a number of obviously hostile questions.

I walked to the parking lot with the university man. We kidded about the difference in audience reaction. Each of us knew that the response grew, in part, out of deep-seated feeling having little to do with the delivery of the speeches, but rather the subject matter involved. He bade me good night saying that the economic intelligence of the average business executive was pretty deplorable. He was confident, however, that time would change all of this because every student to pass the basic economics course at the University had to understand the benefits and necessity of deficit spending.

It occurred to me as I drove home that the professor's parking-lot logic left something to be desired. Of the business executives in the room that evening I would bet that few, if any, were noncollege men. I knew some of them personally. Since they were nearly all under 45 years of age, quite likely the economic training they received was about the same as presently taught at all the better universities. If today's businessman isn't convinced fiscal policy is good, there is little reason to believe tomorrow's executive will be so persuaded.

The fact is, it is truly remarkable that college teaching since the late 1930s has condoned and advocated active use of fiscal policy without making any really lasting impression on students as reflected by their leanings in their executive years. Is this because fiscal policy has been tried and found wanting, or because even though fiscal policy works well it does not redound to the benefit of the business community; or is it

explainable only in terms of business' deep visceral prejudices against deficits and public indebtedness?

Perhaps, the business community would admit that its
dislike for fiscal policy grows out of all three of the possibilities just mentioned. In any event, clearly no progress will be
made repeating all the old arguments about the worth of
fiscal policy. Instead it might be better to concentrate attention in this chapter on where the business community stands
today in relation to it, and to see if there are any changes
which might make it more acceptable to businessmen and
more effective in nurturing a growing economy.

It is probably safe to say that fiscal policy is the favorite
weapon of the economist for dealing with economic ills, just
as monetary policy is the choice of the businessman. Oversimplified, the case for fiscal policy says that a modern economy
is infinitely healthier when there is more spending than
when there is less; so, the government should spend money
to insure health. In the spending of money, government
should try to use funds that otherwise might be idle, and even
pump into the economy some that were not there before—create new money. Out of this simple proposition,
economists have evolved quite a superstructure.

The businessman acknowledges the more spending the
better the economic health of a society, but denies that long-
run good can come from spoon-feeding demand. Businessmen say that when demand declines it means that a society
has momentarily lost its appetite for goods and services. Real
demand won't be restored by stuffing unwanted goods and
services down the throat of a reluctant people. Appetites will
sharpen with a little hunger and the new products and prices
that a bit of adversity will call forth.

The reasoning of most economists leads them to advocate increases in government spending whenever demand falters, and reliance on steeply progressive income taxes to get most of the funds. The poorer members of the community will spend in any event it is assumed, but the rich have so much that some of it may be saved in such a manner as not to find its way back into the spending stream. This leads to the use of deficits whenever the economy goes into recession or growth lags behind the rate commensurate with full employment.

The businessman reasons from different premises. He sees government spending as a part of the overall overhead cost of business. Like all other costs, he wants to hold this one to a minimum. He prefers to pay in taxes each year for whatever government services are absolutely essential. He will go along with progressive taxation, though not at such a steep rate as usually imposed. Deficit financing is repugnant to him, because it tends to conceal from the unsophisticated the true burden of government spending.

Unfortunately, the deep difference between economists and businessmen in approach to fiscal policy has led each camp to make some pretty wild claims. Economists have seemed to aver that all the problems of a modern industrial society can be cured by intelligent use of fiscal policy. Businessmen have trapped themselves by taking such a doctrinaire attitude against deficits and government debt, that it could probably truly be said that if their proposals were enacted the nation would go almost immediately into its most severe postwar depression.

It would be only fair to observe that on paper the economists have had the better of the arguments. Time after time in oral and written debate, economists advocating aggressive use of fiscal policy have proved their point with logic. Never, however, have they convinced the businessman. To him the notion that government spending can do anything more than give a temporary, artificial lift to the economy does not ring true. That the economist should outpoint the business leader in a verbal duel is not surprising. Economists are, after all, purveyors of words. What is more interesting is whether or not fiscal policy has proved itself in actual practice.

Forgetting the outrageous aspects of the arguments made by economists and business leaders it is possible to come to some sort of evaluation of fiscal policy as it is being used in the United States. Clearly, some of the potential "dangers" that businessmen foresaw in the 1930s connected with the use of government spending to stabilize economic conditions have in fact eventuated.

Businessmen warned that government spending would beget government spending; that like a drug it would be habit-forming and require larger dosage to satisfy the need; that withdrawal would be painful if not impossible. In large measure, at least, this warning was prophetic. Today the economy of the United States is much more dependent on government spending than most economists predicted it would be.

At the present time some 9 million civilians, or one person out of eight in the civilian labor force, work for the government. What is more, Victor K. Heyman in a study for the Brookings Institution finds that the time is fast approaching "when employees of the Federal government, like the classic iceberg, are nine-tenths invisible." He estimated in

1961 that directly and indirectly about one-fourth of the total labor force was supported by all government payrolls and contracts.

The notion economists have that government spending could expand when private spending lags, then contract when private spending zooms ahead, has never seemed to work in practice. Once government spending assumes new proportions within the total economy, it seems to remain fixed at that level or to go higher. Only after unusual wartime spending does the government sector seem able to shrink without occasioning recessive forces. This behavior tends to fortify the notion businessmen have that government spending acts as a kind of narcotic to the economy.

From the first, too, business has warned that artificially feeding purchasing power to the economy would sap strength in the long run. While this charge has not been conclusively proved, it is true that a kind of "permanent welfare society" has developed in many major metropolitan areas. Families are reared on welfare payments and seem to go on living that way into succeeding generations. Also there is little doubt that there exists today much more of a tendency to look to Washington for a solution to problems. Individuals, business units, schools, local and state government units all turn to the Federal government for answers that were formerly worked out at a lower level.

Of course, many of the exaggerated charges, such as "we are spending our way to the poorhouse" and "shackling our children with the debt of their fathers," look foolish with hindsight. Nonetheless, interest payments on the government debt are coming to be a real force in their own right. Our failure to balance the budget and to pay for the costs of defending ourselves and the free world in the postwar period through 1957 would seem inexcusable in retrospect. Private demand was generally excessive over this period. To have supplemented it with deficit spending hardly conforms with the "Puritan ethic" that some claim to observe. In any event, with private demand less strong our society must make interest payments on the debt partially established in this former period of redundant spending.

It is disappointing, too, that government spending, which supposedly can be used delicately to compensate for departures from normal in business activity, has been as much a source of short-run instability in the economy as any other single factor since the end of World War II. A case can be made that the recessions of 1953-54 and 1957-58 were caused by ill-timed cuts in expenditures and obligational authority.

Earlier parts of this book, particularly Chapters 5 and 6, have mentioned other disadvantages associated with more frequent intrusion of the Federal government into the workings of the economy—rigidities, imbalances, etc.

If the business community can claim prescience with respect to some of the problems just mentioned, it must also acknowledge the achievements flowing from fiscal policy that it denied would ensue. The overriding achievement involves the prevention of that which first called fiscal policy into use in this country, depression. Even businessmen agree overwhelmingly that the very enormity of government spending has provided and will continue to provide a barrier precluding another major depression in the United States. Bad timing of changes in government spending may have been a cause of business-cycle disturbance in the periods mentioned, but the total volume of this spending and the inbred countercyclical nature of government income and outgo have limited the amplitude of any deviations.

The "automatic stabilizers" built into the government's fiscal operations have proved powerful indeed in the postwar period. When total income declines, the progressiveness of the income tax structure works to reduce tax payments more rapidly. Meanwhile transfer payments, such as unemployment compensation, are rising. These structural offsets work in the other direction too, causing taxes to rise faster and transfer payments to diminish as total income rises.

Like it or not, Federal government spending stands impervious to the onslaught of forces that affect every other type of expenditure. Businessmen never tire of comparing Federal government operations to those of a corporation or even a family; this is transparent nonsense, and most of the businessmen who make these analogies know it. They do it to influence public opinion, and thereby to impose some sort of discipline on the Federal government. It is difficult for me to be too critical of them for this attempt. The power of the Federal government to do good or evil to our business system is infinite. Be assured, however, that just as there are vital biological differences between men and women, though each is a human being, so too are there fundamental dissimilarities between the Federal government and any other spending unit. The Federal government can, after all, create money. No other spenders can make that claim.

This difference enables Federal spending to go upward in the face of the most depressing conditions imaginable. (Conversely, it should be able to resist boom psychology, but it has not exhibited imperviousness in this direction too frequently.) Needless to say the knowledge that Federal spending can and will be used to counter a downtrend in the economy makes somewhat more stable other forms of spending as well.

This means that the American people through huge government expenditures have achieved a measure of the security they have sought so assiduously for the past generation or so. They have gained this security at the price of a measure of freedom, and a little self-respect. For the businessman this price seems prohibitive; for most of the rest of our society it seems small indeed. Thus it is probably safe to say that government expenditures of present proportions are here to stay. The question remains, Can fiscal policy do any more than it has to solve economic ills—can it, for example, speed growth?

At present, fiscal theorists are claiming that a different Federal budget concept would help fiscal policy work better, and perhaps would sit better with the business community. The administrative budget used most commonly in this country is said to be misleading. They say it is erroneously used to weigh the impact of Federal operations on the economy when really it is a tool of program management to keep individual bureaus and departments from spending more money than Congress intends.

In particular, it seems the administrative budget is bad because it is most likely to show a deficit. Experts have estimated that "real" deficits in the recent past and "actual" surpluses have been underreported by an average of about $3 billion a year, largely because the administrative budget excludes multibillion dollar operations of the Social Security and highway trust funds, but includes as expenditures several billion dollars of loans that will be repaid.

The cash budget is the next step along the path of fiscal sophistication. It is used more each year by the periodicals as the best measure of government activities. It presents a more comprehensive view of the money exchange between the Federal government and the public. The cash budget was conceived to pull the overall total of tax receipts and Federal expenditures—including the trust funds excluded by the administrative budget—together.

Fiscal theorists are disturbed by the fact that the administrative budget and the cash budget treat loans as ordinary expenditures, "whereas they have a quite different economic effect." In addition, both register tax receipts on a "when received" basis, yet the economic impact occurs when corporations and individuals set liabilities aside for payment later.

Thus, now there is an attempt to make more use of the accounts prepared by the Commerce Department to measure national income. The national income budget includes government trust funds, excludes loans, purchases of land, and other existing assets, and treats tax liabilities on an accrual basis.

The latest style in fiscal sophistication is the so-called capital budget. This has been around for a long time and is used by many industrialized nations in other parts of the world. The idea is that current operating expenditures, such as wages, should be separated from capital expenditures, such as buildings. Normally the expectation would be that the budget would be in balance if receipts covered current operating expenditures. In the past, conservatives such as Robert Taft and the Hoover Commission have backed the notion of a budget divided between current and capital expenditures.

This concept has a certain built-in appeal to the business community growing from the analogy with sound corporate practice. After all, business does not lump its current costs and capital spending together, and show a loss or deficit merely because in constructing a new factory its expenditures exceeded its income.

As was noted before, however, there are decisive differences between the Federal government and all other spending units, including corporations. For one, government capital facilities, unlike those of private business, do not normally bring an eventual return flow of money income. After all, ordinarily there is no direct charge for government services. Most important, however, is the vital distinction mentioned earlier. Federal government spending is not limited by the normal influences determining business decisions. Its spending potential is limitless. Since increases in spending are associated with good times, it is easy to jump to the conclusion that government should ensure perpetual prosperity by raising its expenditures each year by large amounts. Of course, if this were all that is needed to have a healthy, prospering economy, there would be no sick ones in the world—and some of the sickest should be healthiest. Nevertheless, many within our society cannot resist the temptation to have the government try to spend them into perpetual prosperity. If the capital budget concept were to be widely used in this country, quite probably a little more resistance would crumble.

If you add up the foregoing, it should be evident that I am not too concerned whether it is true that use of the administrative or cash budget "crimps" fiscal policy somewhat. Government services appear to many in our society to be free when no direct charge is made or tax paid. Until there is common understanding that a price is being paid, no matter how concealed, it is probably best that at least we go around burdened by the knowledge that we are unable to balance the budget.

There are, however, changes in fiscal policies that could yield beneficial results in the years ahead. To some extent, these changes are already in process.

It is my opinion that a national consensus is forming to the effect that fiscal policy cannot and should not be readjusted to meet each cyclical swing in the economy. The postwar period has revealed that the very mechanics of government tax-and-spend policy prohibit delicate use of this tool. Congressional machinery is just too cumbersome to make fiscal adjustments precisely timed to match swings in business activity. Reliance should rest squarely upon the automatic stabilizers to offset short-run fluctuations. These, by their very nature, operate countercyclically, and have proved highly effective. Of course, anything "built in" this way should be watched closely and strengthened when necessary.

The business cycle itself takes place within a larger setting. It is the forces in this larger setting that determine long swings in the economy. Such things as trends in the "age mix" within the population, the existence or absence of "pent-up" demand, important new inventions or processes opening up vast new industries, military tensions affecting defense spending, and economic developments in the rest of the world are among what is meant by "forces in the larger setting." It now seems that purposeful, nonautomatic changes in fiscal policy might be made with a view toward the direction those deep-set forces are giving the economy rather than by trying to respond to more shifty, ethereal, cyclical changes.

What this means is that major modifications in the concept of appropriate fiscal policy should be and to some extent are taking place. Conceptually at least, up until now fiscal theorists have promulgated the notion that the idea is to run deficits during recessions, and surpluses when things are booming. Theoretically, this is supposed to balance out over the cycle. Now what is called for is a net surplus for the cycles occurring during the long phase when forces in the larger setting are providing great demand-strength to overall business activity. Net deficits are appropriate over the cycles that comprise the downbeat.

In terms of actual experience, the new concept would have asked a net surplus of tax receipts over Federal expenditures in the postwar period through 1957. Presumably, this would have been achieved by establishing a tax rate high enough to yield a surplus when business activity was booming that would more than offset the deficit involved as the economy passed through the down phase of the short cycle. Such a policy would have been expected to have enabled growth to occur without building into the economy the inflationary bias that originated with excessive demand.

Since 1957 a tax system designed to yield a smaller surplus in up years, and thus a larger net deficit over the several short cycles experienced recently, would have offset weakness in the larger setting.

This thinking represents no small change in fiscal concept. The more common fiscal policy approach to economic problems takes longer-run growth for granted, and is specifically designed to straighten out the recessions that periodically interrupt growth. The primary aim of policy-makers is to set in motion a timely antirecession policy; long-run growth will take care of itself. The "larger setting" approach emphasizes the need to promote long-run growth in its own right. The recessions themselves come to be of secondary importance.

As was noted in Chapter 7 the business community, ostensibly at least, is not as "growth conscious" as others within the American society. For this reason, and because the immediate prescription of the new fiscal appoach involves a series of deficits, businessmen are expected to offer resistance. Thus, little is being said about the new concept by fiscal authorities. Instead, an attempt is being made to write it into legislation on a piecemeal basis. Arguments are waged in traditional terms. Tax cuts are asked to avoid recessions; spending rises are sought for defense purposes, and educational facilities.

Actually, the "larger setting" approach to fiscal policy should sit fairly well with the business community once it is clearly formulated and "batted around." Businessmen are made uneasy by vicissitudes in government policy. The new concept promises a more permanent fiscal stance.

As long, however, as the business community continues to assume a conflict of interest exists between the public and private sectors of the economy, fiscal policy will be handicapped in bringing about a solution to economic problems. The economist sees government and business as institutions of social usefulness which should be permitted to fulfill their functions without being hampered by mutual suspicion. Government activity is good for business activity and vice versa. Businessmen say that private enterprise is the only efficient and "sound" means for attaining national growth.

As an example of what they mean, economists point to the

interrelationship of government and business in technological developments. Gerhard Cohn, Chief Economist of the National Planning Association, has observed that: "The very large government outlays for research and development, particularly in the fields of defense, atomic energy, and space exploration, are creating an enormous reservoir of knowledge and experience in virtually every branch of science and engineering. Private enterprise can tap these resources for the creation of new work materials, new methods of production and management, and new end products. Promotion of a more rapid 'spillover' of technology from the public into the private sector is a challenge to both."

The business community recognizes this challenge, sees the benefits that could develop therefrom, but can't help fearing the long-run consequences of the whole development. As businessmen see it government is too huge, too omnipotent to be a partner. Government, according to this view, is trying to "get in" through the back door—financing research, holding the outstanding scientific brains on its payroll directly or indirectly. Once in, government must dominate and replace other forms of spending and enterprise. Despite the apparent ability of government and private interests to work together profitably in foreign companies such as Volkswagen, the American businessman remains convinced that it cannot, or should not, happen here.

Certainly, if the business community were to accept more of a "mixed" economic system, a good theoretical case could be made for fiscal policy aiding growth in the near future. Government programs of training to raise productivity, policies to improve educational facilities, spending to create job opportunities all could be designed to enlarge incomes of the 20 million or so members of our population at the bottom of the income ladder. In this segment of the population a very large potential market exists for housing, "standard luxuries," cars, and furniture—the commodities for which demand has been relatively slow for the past five years or so.

The economist and fiscal theorist cannot see why businessmen oppose these government programs since they would ultimately benefit from them. To the business community it is like losing a battle to win a war. To the extent that businessmen permit government to "solve" this problem for them they weaken the basic strength of the American system, and in the long run do harm, not good.

Another change in the conception of fiscal policy seems to be emerging. Up until now it has been the practice to quantitatively relate government spending to growth. In crudest terms, the economic assumption has been, the more government spending, the more growth. Only the business community has demurred.

Now that fiscal theorists are coming to look beyond cyclical policy, however, and are thinking in terms of forces in the larger setting influencing longer-run trends, there is more of a tendency to study qualitatively the pattern of government spending. No longer is the concern merely how much government spending will help growth, but what kind. Much is being said in connection with finding a new "galvanizing force" to stimulate activity throughout the economy. The one mentioned most frequently is a huge national program of urban redevelopment. Certainly, in this area active government leadership is needed, and, if successful, extraordinary opportunities for the business community will open up.

Notwithstanding the reasonableness of "selecting" a galvanizing force—in the past they weren't planned—the trend toward qualitative evaluations of government spending is a hopeful sign. It has long seemed strange that economists equated—insofar as their economic impact is concerned—expenditures for armaments, for example, and, say, schools. True enough, the funds paid for materials and labor in each instance generate income in like amounts throughout the economy. The difference is that schools yield a return flow of services over a long period. Unless there is war, spending for armament stops yielding returns once paid for.

In summary, I would stand on what I said earlier: the economist has presented his case more logically and persuasively. Yet, so much of the economic case looks better on paper than it works out to be in actual fact; so much yields benefits in the short run, but exacts a tremendous price in sapping long-run strength. It is unfortunate, I suppose, that people will not give their best unless compensated appropriately, that sometimes adversity provides more motivation than affluence; but whether or not unfortunate, it is true. The economist in making his case frequently loses sight of such fundamentals. To the businessman they are all-important.

Perhaps the most hopeful sign is that fiscal policy-makers have directed their attention to growth. Since first used in the 1930s, Federal tax-and-spend policies have been preoccupied with the problem of full employment. Of course, as recent British experience demonstrates, full employment does not automatically generate a growth rate commensurate with a prospering healthy economy. Assuring healthy growth is more complicated than this. While the business community has made a lot of bad arguments along the way, maybe this is what it has been trying to say for a long time.

11

Controls, Antitrust Guides, and Devaluation

Part 2 of this book has discussed, so far, growth and those public policies that might contribute to it. Planning, monetary policy, and fiscal policy have all been around for quite some time. Each is changing to meet the new requirements of the times. Nonetheless, there is a strong feeling within the business community and elsewhere that something more is needed to get the economy moving.

To be sure, planning seems to be helping some European countries to grow rapidly. The American businessman, I have alleged, abhors planning. Quite likely his strong feeling and the inbred antipathy toward planning shared by most of the rest of his countrymen will preclude its use here. Monetary policy is looked on with favor by the businessman. But expansionary monetary policy to promote growth has had to be—and in the near future probably will have to be—modified out of regard for the fact that low interest rates would ensue and aggravate balance-of-payments and gold outflow problems. Federal Reserve people themselves say it has done just about all that it can to promote enlarged demand. Businessmen are far from partial to fiscal policy. By now, however, the business community has resigned itself to it. Heavy government expenditures do form a bulwark against a depression. In the current economic environment it is difficult to see how fiscal policy can speed growth to the level of full employment without bringing on price rises that will aggravate our foreign payments problems.

Of course, not everyone agrees with these assessments. For the most part, this is the thinking of the business community. Leon Keyserling, Chairman of the Council of Economic Advisers under President Truman, for example, feels that a really substantial increase in government spending and a good-sized tax cut would solve the problems of growth and foreign payments. Notwithstanding some disagreement, there is a good chance the business community is right this time.

No less an authority than the late Per Jacobsson, eminent economist and Managing Director of the International Monetary Fund, in 1963 in the Arthur K. Salomon lecture at New York University, said: "Let me begin with the cost factor and state here and now that moderation in cost increases is the right policy, both in order to stimulate growth internally and to improve the balance of payments position." Neither monetary policy nor fiscal policy seems able to be of decisive influence on costs or prices except at the expense of lagging growth and excessive unemployment. Mr. Jacobsson felt that monetary and fiscal policies had roles to play in getting America growing at a healthy pace again, but that the effort would be largely wasted if costs and prices could not be controlled. There has to be some kind of what in Europe is now referred to as an "incomes policy." An incomes policy, in simplest terms, is nearly anything that works to hold labor costs and prices in line.

Paying attention to costs comes naturally to the businessman. He is heartened that others are beginning to share his concern. To date, however, no consensus has formed around a policy to bring costs into line. Instead recognition of the problem is forging a kind of discipline of its own. An improvised hand of accepted procedure is evolving and restraining costs and prices otherwise free from market control.

For the most part, the improvised hand is a compromise, not a policy. If it is working at present it is uneven in its impact, effective only if accompanied by lagging growth and excessive unemployment, and largely unrecognized as to its existence. For these reasons the search is still on for a policy or policies that will hold costs and prices stable even while the economy is growing rapidly at full employment.

At first blush it would seem that there should be easier, more certain means of controlling costs and prices than through an improvised hand. There are. Perhaps most direct, price and wage controls could be tried. It says a lot to observe that no consideration whatever is being given to introducing a policy of price- and wage-fixing, although, theoretically at least, it would seem worthy of consideration. Without going into all the other disadvantages, maybe it is enough to say that no one believes the American people would settle for such a procedure except in the event of real and obvious crisis, such as war or other calamity.

Price controls ordinarily are used only to repress strong inflationary pressures as a result of tremendously excessive demand. To be effective they must be accompanied by rationing. The latter creates many administrative and enforcement problems. The entire price control policy involves elimination of the price mechanism as the device controlling distribution of goods among various buyers. It is essentially a last-resort method.

The businessman has his own "quick cure" for what ails us. He would break up unions. He is is not advocating complete dissolution of the union movement, rather fragmentization of the great labor monopolies. Insofar as unions can be divested of monopolistic power and operate as small independent units, they can remain free to bargain and to strike. In the eyes of the business community, labor monopolies have abused the power they were ceded in the 1930s to meet big industry on equal terms. It is these strong unions, with their demands for wage increases even in the face of an unfavorable market environment, who have removed costs and prices from any systematic causation. If monopolistic unions are slivered, costs will stop rising and prices will fall into line.

The businessman does not push his fragmentization recommendations too hard, however, for fear they might catch on and spread. Though not sophisticated politically, the businessman instinctively senses that if government were to undertake to fracture huge unions it would have to do the same to big industry. There are those within government whose responsibilities cause them to think in this direction in any event. In addition, on many small college campuses it is still possible to find academicians who feel that big unions and big business should be broken up, and perfect competition restored. Lack of broad public support inhibits action. The businessman wants to keep it that way.

In a way it is surprising that businessmen are now and always have been so dead set against "trust-busting." They would agree that the most valuable kind of planning is what has been called unplanning—the establishment of institutions in such a way that government is able to permit free forces to regulate and direct activity. Antitrust legislation was conceived and generally has been carried out in this spirit; still the business community has opposed it bitterly.

This may seem natural enough in the sense that no one cheers the umpire or referee. The businessman's distaste is not so easily explainable. No one, especially the participants, would deny the need for umpires in a baseball game. Businessmen would and do deny the need for antitrust activity. The market game, they say, requires no referee.

Their logic, in view of the obvious near-monopolistic power some have, is explainable only in terms of their schizophrenia, discussed earlier. Businessmen love the market game, but a part of that game is to try to beat the market. Another part of their faith says that it can't be beaten, and this is why it is right that they should try so hard. For the businessman to admit that antitrust activity is necessary and desirable is tantamount to acknowledging that the market system does not really work.

Businessman opposition is far from the only reason why there will be some talk, but really very little antitrust action to bring costs and prices back under the sway of market forces. The American people in general have mixed emotions about bigness. They fear, respect, and admire it. Out of their fear, the Sherman Act was passed in 1890; because of their respect and admiration, antitrust action has not prevented immense corporate combines from dominating business activity.

It still goes against the grain in this country to take something that was legally won away from someone. Few, if any, of the real corporate empires owe their predominate positions to shady merger machinations. Nearly all started small and made good in competition with their rivals at every level on the way up. If they gobbled up competitors through merger, it was after "softening" them up in battle. If they purchased smaller suppliers, it was out of profits earned in the marketplace. They are products of the American enterprise system. It does not seem right to most people to penalize them for their success.

Most important is that to attempt to restore supremacy to the market would be to move contrary to long-standing and seemingly irresistible forces. Time was when a nimble liberal could make a beautiful case surrounding the general notion that the big cannot be free; that the prizes of competition had to be limited or in the end freedom itself would be destroyed. He won nearly all the scholastic debates. In the real world he lost nearly all the battles, and the war.

Time after time he was able to prove with facts, figures, and cogent analysis that firms did not have to be nearly so big as some were to achieve all the economies of scale, that size was being sought for the market power it bestowed. Whether or not right, the fight is over. The public just was not interested. Bigness is here to stay.

Yet antitrust proceedings continue. If antitrust will not bring prices and costs under market control, is it an anachronism that will pass as more come to recognize what has already taken place? I think not. The spirit of antitrust has a place in American society. If it has not preserved mastery for the marketplace, it has restrained big firms from abusing the mastery they have assumed. The fact of antitrust legislation and the will to use it can be most important ingredients in the fashioning of an improvised hand.

In an earlier chapter I suggested that it was bad for the American business system that some firms were afraid to get bigger proportionally. Afraid, not because it would lead to inefficiency, rather because it might bring antitrust action. My suggestion was that the business community recognize this and appoint a commission of its own to ferret out situations of this sort—no firm should fear increasing its share of the market.

I stand on that suggestion. Nonetheless, I am realistic enough to understand that my proposal may never be heeded. Very little in the past history of the business community indicates that it will be anxious to "police" itself. What this means is that the Attorney General could take the lead in appointing such a commission of citizens: first, to formulate broad philosophy, and later to impose its interpretations back onto the business community.

The formulation of this philosophy could start with the assumption that no attempt would be made to restore "perfect competition." This is, after all, a meaningless abstraction in a world of manufacturing plants representing a heavy permanent investment, and on whose stability depends the security of thousands. There would be an attempt to assure that competition was sufficient so that each firm in the industry was unafraid to grow larger, and that consumers were enjoying most of the benefits which competition is supposed to afford.

It would be possible to get really excited about gaining some sort of improvised market control over prices if labor costs were showing more responsiveness to this kind of persuasion. The temptation is to say that the Antitrust Division could, at the very least, harass and inhibit huge union concentrations by questioning their legitimate need for such monopolistic power. This might "force" more appropriate behavior upon labor. Actually, I would not be too hopeful about progress in this direction.

For one thing it would be extremely difficult to carry off from a political standpoint. More to the point, though, it would smack of a new attempt to restore balance between corporate and union power. Better that big labor and big industry are not trimmed to each other's size. Society might delude itself once more into believing that, upon restoration of balance, countervailing power would insure that general good would rise out of the competition between big labor and big business.

The very obviousness of the economic power vested in the leaders of large unions should make for responsible behavior. Labor must come to realize what corporate behemoths finally understand: that huge, powerful units cannot compete for everything they can get. When they do the public, indeed the nation, gets hurt.

Mutual recognition of the preceding could go a long way toward "civilizing" labor. Once the whole idea of countervailing power for big labor and big industry is discarded, progress can be made. Labor, after all, is a part of the firm, just as stockholders are a part. Labor is a part of the firm which, because of its economic power, can do much harm or good. Business should be able to expect labor to want to do good.

But business cannot expect labor to sit back and be told what its duty consists of. The quickest way to get labor leaders to accept responsibility is to give it to them. Labor must be brought into the boardroom. It is my guess that 25 years from now all the huge industries owned by masses of stockholders will have maybe 12 directors, with three appointed by the stockholders, three from management, three from labor, and three representing the public at large. The directors would not act in the narrow sense of being representatives of labor, management, etc., but would be symbolic reminders of the centers of interest.

In the meantime, progress will be slow. Some firms will move faster than others in bringing labor into the "show." Many will continue to "countervail" with unions in the dated manner, and some unions will remain suspicious.

Attempts have been made by the government to direct labor along the path toward respectable, responsible use of its economic power. In the Economic Report of the President for 1962, guidelines were laid down that purported to provide appropriate wage-rise demands. The idea was to tie wage boosts to the overall improvement in productive efficiency, which averages about $2\frac{1}{2}$ to 3 per cent a year.

Briefly, the reasoning was that wage demands of the various unions should hover around 3 per cent. At this level most industries could absorb the increase without raising prices. Some industries have yearly increases in efficiency well beyond 3 per cent. They would be able to reduce prices. In other industries efficiency doesn't increase enough to justify the wage hike without a price rise. That would be all right since they would be offset by the price declines in the more efficient sector.

Unfortunately, as is the case with many mathematically precise, theoretically logical answers to economic problems, this one did not work. Some unions paid no attention to the prescription. Many others did, but chose to interpret it to mean that additions to fringe benefits did not count in the 3 per cent computation. Businessmen were unenthusiastic from the start. To them the guideline idea represented "an ivory tower solution that took little cognizance of actual problems." Putting their case as succinctly as possible: businessmen thought it foolish to imply that firms in booming, stagnating, growing, declining, new, and old industries should be subject to uniform wage pressures.

Of course, what in the eyes of some is the quickest, surest, easiest method of getting costs and prices in line has not even been discussed as yet—devaluation of the dollar. Gold does not circulate internally, but is used to settle balances among nations. Europe resumed convertibility in 1958. It is not entirely coincidental that 1958 was the year the United States began really noticing its payments gap.

Devaluation can be accomplished by revaluing United States money in terms of gold. For example, this country could begin paying $70 an ounce for gold instead of $35. Theoretically, this should have no effect on domestic costs and prices, but would roughly halve United States costs and prices as compared with the rest of the world.

It is no secret that, from the end of World War II to the

present, wage costs have been relatively high in the United States as compared with Western Europe. For a decade high costs here were obscured by Europe's lack of productive capacity. Since Europe completed reparations on its damaged industrial plants and resumed convertibility, this cost differential has assumed increasing importance.

The gold exchange standard now in use compels a country to become more competitive if it wants to eliminate deficits in its payments to the rest of the world. Under the old-fashioned gold standard, countries had a nearly automatic remedy for persistent payments gaps. The gold outflow would shrink the money supply, deflation would ensue and bring costs below those of other countries. Now the adjustment is no longer spontaneous. Governments are not willing to accept the unemployment that accompanies deflation. Partly as a result, prices and wages are too rigid to drop much.

This seems to require a country to devalue or to sit back and wait for costs in the rest of the world to climb to competitive levels. In the case of the United States there are those who allege that we have been sitting back long enough, that it is time to devalue.

Needless to say the businessman is not in favor of devaluation. His doubts as to the efficacy of this move are manifold. A look at the past tells him that in the event of devaluation domestic costs probably will rise despite the theoretical logic which says they should not. The whole idea of devaluation relaxes, psychologically at least, discipline and provides a backdrop for rising prices. There is a lot of anticipatory buying and general frenzy in capital markets. In addition, the businessman knows there is some chance that this will set in motion competitive devaluations in the currencies of other foreign nations which may eventually nullify the move here.

Most of all, however, the businessman sees devaluation as the wrong medicine at the wrong time; so wrong that it might not only fail to cure, it might do harm. Costs in this country vis-à-vis the rest of the world have been fairly high for a long time—maybe since before World War I. Historically, America has competed effectively by producing quality goods and through innovation—we can make some things the rest of the world wants even at high prices.

Unquestionably, other parts of the world have made headway in catching up to us on these counts. That we still have a margin of superiority when challenged is attested to by the way our auto makers turned back the foreign car once they set their minds to it. It is more in keeping with tradition and with the kind of society we want to maintain that we stay ahead in quality and innovation, rather than by cutting costs with financial gimmickry. American businessmen believe that there will be a flagging of spirit if once more the "painless" answer is pursued.

On the other hand, businessmen believe that the United States payments gap is saying something that America must heed; something that devaluation will hide, but not cure. It is not saying just that costs and prices are high, it is saying that this nation is assuming a larger position in world affairs than we as a people want to occupy. Since 1957, events have conspired in such a way as to begin to make us aware that this is the case.

From the end of World War II to the present, Americans have been asked by their leaders to share their wealth and know-how with the world. In a way that no other people before approached, this sharing has taken place. This is to our everlasting credit. But let it be said in all truth that over much of this period—until about 1957—a few important factors were at work which helped us go along with the assumption of the burden.

Perhaps most important, Europe and the rest of the world were in such obvious need of help as a result of war devastation as to call forth the best in us. There was also the feeling that if we did not help, Russia and Communism would overtake the world. Communism spreads fastest among the sick. The United States felt it had to help the world get well. Then, too, in this country economic growth was coming easily and rapidly. Living standards were rising faster even than the indexes revealed. It is not so hard to give a significant slice when the pie itself gets larger each year.

Finally, inflation was disguising in part what was happening. Despite all that might be said to be wrong with inflation, the truth is that, so long as it does not run wild, most people prefer it to paying higher taxes. Of course, it is less obvious than taxation, but in the years after World War II it has had a similar effect. It diverted resources from consumers and businessmen to the government sector.

In sum then, Americans assumed a generous attitude toward the rest of the world because it seemed the right thing; it was in our own best interest and because we seemed able to have the penny and the cake both—able to subsidize the Free World and to enjoy a rapidly rising standard of living.

Over the past few years, on the other hand, much has changed. The Free World is no longer obviously in need of help; Communism seems to have lost much of its appeal, and does not loom so portentous; economic growth is not coming easily or rapidly here; and inflation no longer masks the burden of defending and caring for the Free World.

This means that defense and foreign affairs costs carried by this country seem magnified as ameliorating factors fade. Taxes loom larger since they are no longer supplemented by inflation. John F. Kennedy revealed that he saw what was happening when in early speeches after being elected he called for sacrifices. Unfortunately, however, the late President never quite spelled the whole thing out clearly enough for the broad public to understand.

The business community likes the fact that the real burden we are carrying is finally showing through. Businessmen believe that in this environment Americans are more likely to cut back what is not most necessary, likely to eliminate wasteful foreign aid. This, after all, is what the situation does seem to call for. Exports exceed imports, but foreign aid, military spending overseas, and investment flowing abroad more than make up the difference.

There is yet another strong reason why devaluation is not an appropriate "incomes policy" for the United States at this time. It grows out of the fact that for some time now the dollar has been as "good as gold"—used instead of gold as a supplementary medium of exchange. Central banks of the various nations have used the dollar to pay debts to one another—as if it were gold. Naturally, if dollars were devalued they would cease to be used as a substitute world medium of exchange. Right now dollars constitute about half of Free World monetary reserves (outside the United States). Dollars would go out of style fast if devalued, and the world would accelerate its demand for United States gold. Central banks would cease to use the dollar as a reserve currency. In a sense then, devaluation might accentuate the gold outflow problem.

In summary, the United States finds itself in need of a policy that would hold costs and prices in line while expansionary monetary and fiscal policy bring the economy to a position of full employment and near-capacity utilization of productive plant. Theoretically, at least, a number of moves could be attempted such as: direct price and wage controls; vigorous antitrust action to try to restore "perfect competition" in commodity and labor markets; "guidelines" to regulate wages and then prices; and devaluation which could drastically reduce costs and prices as compared with other countries.

Each of these moves has serious disadvantages. Price and wage controls or devaluation are so contrary to our traditions as to be used only in the event of extreme emergency. Antitrust action has a place, but really it is a little late to go back to where for some time we have not been and where few really want to go. Guidelines have been tried without notable success.

Instead of any of these, a kind of self-discipline might be evolving. In an earlier chapter I said that the businessman's complex, contradictory actions and theorizing about the American business system are leading to an improvised hand of accepted procedure to replace the former invisible hand of competition. Unfortunately, the new discipline seems only able to hold costs and prices in line at unsatisfactory levels of employment, growth, and profits. The discipline seems to work only if accompanied by some pain. Methods of improving its effectiveness and removing the discomfort should be explored. A commission of businessmen to help "clear the air" on antitrust might be helpful. Recognizing labor as a part of the firm could serve to cause unions to accept all the responsibility their economic power demands.

The businessman understands the need for something in addition to fiscal and monetary policies. He rejects controls, guidelines, trust-busting, and devaluation. This seems to leave him with the improvised hand. If ways cannot be found to expedite the new hand, it will be only a question of time before a "bold new approach"—such as devaluation—will be foisted onto the economy in an attempt to combine faster growth, full employment, and an end to the payments deficit.

part 3

The Big New Challenges

12

The Peace Scare

The businessman is not so smug and self-satisfied as his critics allege; much of what has been said about him in this book should have made that point clear. There have been times—especially in the 1930s—when his faith wavered, when he felt he was losing his grip, when the situation seemed out of his control, when answers seemed beyond his ken. Now again his confidence is restored, or at least returning.

To be sure, he is not entirely happy about the way things are going. As was noted, especially in Part 1 of this book, the businessman is distressed that labor and government have changed and are changing the American business system, that involuntarily even he traduces it. But he sees himself battling against tremendous odds. Everyone else would "let it all pass into history," would embrace eagerly the welfare state and socialism undiluted, were it not for his influence.

He is more confident than he has been for a decade, or even a generation, that the businessman will remain the leading figure in the economic life of this country and the world. For a time, he really believed the government bureaucrat would replace him.

Despite his relative serenity, the businessman is not without worries—worries growing out of his observation of forces over which he seems able to have little decisive influence. The businessman can visualize certain events, any one of which could raise such huge problems, could cause such profound crises as to change dramatically the economic world in which he lives, possibly, therefore, change him. Part 3 of this book discusses those events which the businessman sees as not too remote, and of potentially far-reaching consequences insofar as his economics are concerned.

*   *   *

It is indeed difficult to imagine what the world would be like if the nation-states within it could not resort to war. How could powerful nations achieve their ends? "War," said Clausewitz, "is not merely a political act, but also a political instrument, a continuation of political relations, a carrying out of the same by other means."

Now there are those who say that, while what Clausewitz said was true for a long time, it is no longer true. That, as a matter of fact, the idea that war is a sane part of overall national policy represents a cultural lag. General Douglas MacArthur told the Philippine Assembly in 1961 that war in the Nuclear Age had lost its meaning. "If you lose you are annihilated. If you win you stand only to lose. . . . It contains now only the germs of a double suicide."

Businessmen think "tougher" than most members of American society. By this I mean that they are less likely to get carried away by idealistic notions, or nice-sounding phrases. But businessmen are coming to the conclusion that disarmament is possible.

In the winter of 1963 I appeared on a TV public affairs show to discuss the economic consequences of disarmament. The moderator began the program by asking the other participant if he thought disarmament was feasible. My fellow responder was an official of the General Electric Company, which, of course, does a lot of defense business. He replied that he did indeed think that disarmament was possible. In general the point made by the G.E. man was that if you can't use military power without its inducing self-annihilation, it is useless.

What seems true today is that the United States and Russia understand this as a fact. Unfortunately, however, neither has been able to work out means of playing power politics other than those appropriate to the pre-1945 world. Political leaders in each country have done business as usual, as if a twenty-megaton bomb were the same as a battleship. Transparently, what the United States and Russia are doing looks more and more like playing charades. All the moves and countermoves are there, but each knows the other won't go to war. It seems inevitable that the nonsense must end and disarmament be accomplished.

It is easy enough to measure arithmetically the impact of disarmament on the American economy. This spending represents more than $55 billion, or about 10 per cent of the gross national product. Of course, this amount would not all be wiped out in any one year; in fact, probably never would it be entirely eliminated. The United States, it is estimated, would probably have to spend something like $10 billion a year for defense even after disarmament is consummated. In effect, what we are talking about is paring defense spending down from about 10 per cent of GNP to 2 per cent. That is quite a drop. Yet, on paper it can easily be compensated for by a tax cut, and increases in other forms of spending.

Actually, however, what happens after disarmament makes a tremendous difference to the American society. More Americans than like to admit it do not believe that we can have prosperity without a heavy load of defense spending. If suspicions were to be confirmed by a spate of bad times, the psychological mood of the nation might be such as to welcome radical change. If, on the other hand, government gets in with all kinds of programs and policies to "insure" the nation against recession subsequent to disarmament, then maybe the system is changed out of fear of what might have happened.

Unfortunately, businessmen have little to say on the matter of policy recommendations in the event of sharp declines in defense spending. For the most part they content themselves with citing the experience following World War II. It does make pretty pleasant reading.

In 1945 the United States was spending about $145 billion on defense. (Everything is in terms of 1960 dollars.) This was cut to $28 billion in 1946. Over this period 9 million men were released from the armed forces, and unemployment stayed below 4 per cent of the labor force. Nearly all of the leading economists at that time predicted a fairly sharp recession during the period of demobilization. They were wrong.

It is misleading, however, to forecast from this experience in trying to visualize conditions following any kind of demobilization in the 1960s, despite the comfort it might bring to reflect over it. Certain crucial factors were at work then that cannot be counted upon in the present or foreseeable circumstances. For example, there developed over the war years a tremendous buildup of demand. Virtually no new automobiles were produced from the end of 1941 through 1945. Many other durable goods were in short supply. Rationing limited purchases. Price controls were the order of the day. In addition, because of price controls, rationing, and high incomes, consumers and corporations built up huge liquid resources. This combination of backed-up demand and redundant savings touched off enough spending to smooth the transition period.

To some extent the fact that the labor force had been under strain during the war period had the effect of ameliorating the adjustment following the drastic slash in military spending. Many overage men had been drawn back into the work force by patriotism and high incomes during the war years. Many wives had worked while their husbands were overseas. This abnormal swelling of the ranks of the working was followed by a kind of painless shrinkage to normal as workers voluntarily left or stayed out of the labor force.

Finally, the psychology of the moment was different then than it is likely to be again soon. The United States was proud of itself and the role industry played in the war effort.

Clearly, we emerged with the world our oyster. Although fear of depression lurked in the subconscious, joy unrestrained was the prevailing mood.

Actually, the demobilization period following the Korean intervention might come closer to approximating the conditions surrounding disarmament when and if it comes. At that time defense expenditures dropped from $62 billion in 1953 to $51 billion in 1954. The decline of the defense effort was not really treated as demobilization requiring strong compensatory action at that time. Taxes were reduced, however, and though 1954 was a recession year the decline in GNP was less than the reduction in defense spending. Unemployment rose to 5.6 per cent of the labor force.

Shortly thereafter defense spending leveled and began rising once more, ending any similarity with conditions probable in the event of disarmament.

The truth is that what happens if we disarm is not foreseeable from past experience. Before about 1940 America was always virtually disarmed except when at war. Since that time we have been armed, only more so when at war. To be sure our industrial system has accommodated itself to the arms race, and in a sense, therefore, has become dependent on it—after all, defense spending has accounted for 9 per cent or more of total spending since 1951. What happens when the prop is taken away?

As is always the case with problems economic, there are short-term and long-term considerations to be taken into account. In the short run the problems boil down to two: (1) how to avoid a slowdown; (2) how to avoid unnecessary waste and suffering as people and capital are shifted to new localities, industries, and types of work.

Avoiding a slowdown would seem to be the easier problem to solve. For technical reasons it might be necessary to stretch out disarmament over a decade as adequate inspection arrangements and reliable enforcement procedures are worked out. This would involve cuts of about $5 billion a year or so for about 10 years. Such a stretch-out should not "shock" the economy too much. It would also enable a little experimentation with compensatory policy. For example, it would be possible to "mix" tax relief and increased spending by government on nondefense in varying proportions.

This is not to say that $5 billion a year is not much; it is. Although less than 1 per cent of GNP, it could have a multiplier effect as those losing jobs, as well as those fearful of becoming unemployed, cut back spending. Following these developments business might cut investment spending, and the stock market could plunge through the floor. There would be, of course, every incentive to forestall such eventualities. Government would have good reason to take strong offsetting actions.

The innate conservatism—"Puritan ethic"—of the American people, fostered by the business community, might play havoc with compensatory policy. A survey group in 1962 asked a sample of Americans what they would recommend the government do in the event of disarmament. The answer given more than any other was, pay off the national debt. Earlier I noted that there is usually resistance to government spending on things other than defense. I believe, however, the actual event of disarmament would be recognizable as an emergency so that there would be sufficient apprehension over business conditions to justify exceptional actions. Tax cuts and increases in other government spending would be sought and granted. It is my view that serious recession would be avoided.

On the other hand, specific hardships and dislocations would be difficult if not impossible to avoid. It is estimated that 95 per cent of all jobs in the aircraft and missile industry, 60 per cent of the jobs in shipbuilding, and 40 per cent in communications equipment depend on defense spending. Much of the defense spending is concentrated in a few areas. California, New York, Massachusetts, and Connecticut would have potentially serious regional problems in the event of disarmament.

Conversion of facilities and personnel might be "sticky." Defense business is like no other. There is just one customer for output. For this reason and others, firms heavily involved in this work generally lack marketing know-how, in the conventional sense at least. Some personnel in these firms may have difficulty applying their skills to regular civilian business in spite of the fact that they work highly efficiently in some aspect of the defense industry.

If, for example, tax cuts were relied upon to increase civilian spending, it is difficult to imagine that corporations and workers deeply committed to defense could benefit in the short run. Just as difficult is it to visualize government spending for nondefense purposes benefiting these firms and their employees. Increases in spending for schools, hospitals, and road-building could be met to only a very limited extent, if at all, by the labor and equipment released from, say, the aircraft and electronic industries, which currently receive a high proportion of defense expenditures going to industry .

What then should be done? Does society have an obligation to the firms and workers unable to move easily from defense to civilian pursuits? To be sure this is the kind of question to which there is no hard and fast answer. On the one hand, a case could be made that the community has no more obligation to this group than it has to any other group made obsolete by changing tastes or technological innovations. Is not the man automated out of a job as much the victim of the fall of the cards as the defense worker? In my view he is. But I don't expect my view to prevail.

Business thought in this area has not crystallized. Instinctively, the businessman reacts schizophrenically. He talks tough and behaves soft. Broadly, he says business must adjust itself, but for his own firm he pleads for special favors. The contradiction doesn't impress him; it has a long history.

It is my guess that society feels that loss of business or job as a result of the capriciousness of consumer tastes or the introduction of new products or processes is a natural hazard of the economic game. As such its consequences must be borne, alleviated only by unemployment compensation and other routine aids to adjustment. Disarmament will be regarded as something quite different. Victims of it will be accorded special treatment for the trick fate has played on them.

The short-run consequences of this generous attitude should help the economy avert recession and serious slowdown. The form this community munificence takes will determine its long-run consequences.

Basically, moves made to lighten the impact of disarmament on particular industries and workers could take two directions. On the one hand, emphasis could be placed on trying to get private spending to expand and replace defense expenditures. In this case tax cuts would be relied on to free income and bring about rises in consumer and business spending. Tax relief should be timed in such a way and be of sufficient magnitude to produce a deficit before decreases in defense spending take their toll on incomes and profits.

Several affected industries would get special tax treatment. Cost of retooling for civilian production, for example, could be minimized by extremely favorable accelerated depreciation provisions. Indirect taxes on the final product could be waived. Possibly, even more exceptional tax treatment could be devised to ease the transition of the defense-committed firm or individual to civilian production. Most likely markets into which producers would turn might include industrial automation equipment, civil aircraft equipment, space research, communications, and consumer durables.

Conceivably, great emphasis could be placed on maintaining income for the affected corporations and jobs and wages for their workers, causing government policy makers to introduce highly unusual programs. For example, maybe if markets were not immediately available for the civilian products of converted defense firms, the government would purchase unwanted products, or guarantee their price as with some farm products.

This general approach might have some appeal to the business community. Presumably, the goal of the relief and government purchases would be to help defense-oriented industry through the interim period of adjustment to useful civilian production. Theoretically, in the long run, the result of this policy would be to reduce dependence of the economy on government spending as firms successfully completed their conversion.

Despite the happy sound of the preceding, such a course of

action is not without disadvantages. To begin with, what start out to be interim periods have a way of turning into interminable periods. Tax concessions, price supports, and the like could easily become permanently grafted onto the converted defense firms. Certainly, it has proved difficult to get rid of parity price supports for farm products. Not much imagination is required to visualize a similar situation here.

Even assuming the interim adjustment could be successfully accomplished, problems remain. Say about it what you will, Federal spending provides stability to the economy. The American business system has tended to harden around a rather heavy load of such spending. Remove a good part of it and some stability must be lost, even if the flexibility imparted may be very healthy to a free-enterprise system. The point is that by now no one can be sure that America has any longer the kind of market system that can respond to this challenge, can make the most of flexibility. To many, a cleaner, more reasonable course of action to meet disarmament would recognize the existing level of defense spending as roughly appropriate, would recognize "the facts of life" insofar as free enterprise is concerned. Barbara Ward, writing in the *Saturday Review,* said in 1962 that: "Above all, the experience of the last decades underlines the fact that private demand alone does not unlock the full range of modern scientific production. . . . On the contrary, resources are limited by scarce imaginations. Yet it is broadly time to say in the West today this freedom of imagination comes only when—as with arms or the space race—fear is involved."

Barbara Ward and many others would use fear of the economic consequences of all-out peace as a weapon to secure assent for wide-ranging Federal programs to replace the defense effort. Instead of trying to cause defense-oriented firms and workers to adjust to the production of civilian gadgets, they would keep them in place working on such problems as urban rehabilitation, desalinization of water, climate control, integration of transportation facilities, population control, etc. If any money, or the willingness to spend, is left over, it could go toward more mundane government operations which heretofore have been "crimped" by the emphasis on defense. Possibly too, the disarmament crisis could provide an opportunity to adjust somewhat the scale of values of the American people. Subsidization of the arts and other "worthwhile" pursuits could be encouraged. The period would probably also afford an excellent climate within which to raise the pay of government workers such as teachers.

No doubt an ambitious program along the course just outlined would preclude much of a slowdown as America adjusted to disarmament. In fact, its short-run advantages would make it difficult to resist. Unfortunately, this course is not without long-run disadvantages. Giving to government responsibility for solving the big problems facing civilization would permanently deflect the best scientific brains away from corporations meeting the market test. Scientific talent would be diverted toward government-oriented industry just as this talent now gravitates to defense-based firms. Even now businessmen claim that new civilian products are not forthcoming because of the quantity and quality of research distracted by more glamorous government assignments.

This could mean that eventually only through government spending could the American economy maintain momentum. Market direction would dominate, perhaps, a proportionately smaller, in any event an obviously less significant, part of the economy.

What this all means, of course, is that problems are involved no matter what the response to disarmament. This is why open discussion of the various courses of action should be encouraged in advance of such an eventuality. The near impossibility of predicting exactly what the course of the economy would be like in disarmament discourages attempts, but they should be made. What comes will depend to some extent on how the economy is going when the peace agreement is reached. If the economy is already a bit slack, as is likely, a more expansionary policy will be pursued.

Under any conditions probable, no administration that I can imagine in office would subject the American economy to the "shock" of a $40 billion or so decline in Federal spending, even if over a five- to ten-year period, without substantial compensating actions. (Politicians who keep pretty closely to the businessman's line of thought have picked up the split personality. Eisenhower's businessman administration was not too different from the Fair Deal and the New Frontier. The tune was about the same, even if some of the lyrics were different.) Any imaginable administration would treat the occasion as a period of economic crisis and adopt emergency measures to preclude serious immediate recession. This means that a policy would be forged from those advocating reliance on tax reduction and those pressing for offsetting increases in other Federal spending. Within the atmosphere that is likely to prevail it will take an exceptional administration to utilize measures during the interim period that do not permanently scar or transform in ugly manner the American business system.

One of the lessons that might profitably have been learned from the past few decades is that "overcuring" can be harmful. In our understandable anxiety to see the economy through disarmament, let us not so protect it that it ceases to be worth protecting.

It would be insane to try to repay the Federal debt with the savings from the reduction in arms spending; every economist and many businessmen recognize this. It would be just as foolish to attempt to disarm without disturbing the rhythm and proportions of the existing industrial order; every businessman and some economists understand this. While it is beyond reason that the former policy will receive serious consideration, it is not at all sure that the latter will be similarly eschewed.

13

Changes in the World Can Change Us

It is so obviously true as to be trite to observe that we live in a changing world. This chapter will not waste time proving what is already known. What is to be probed here is the question: Will this changing world change us? Generally, it is assumed that only if a different economic system demonstrates convincing superiority would the American business system be jeopardized. This may not be true. The businessman wonders whether other foreign events over which we have little or no control won't influence drastically our business society.

Possibly, changes in the rest of the world will be—or have already been—so vast as to cause alterations in our system. Some businessmen are convinced that this is the case. There is little agreement, however, on what world developments are most portentous.

If the businessman is unable to pinpoint the foreign development most likely to threaten his existence, it is no wonder. In the brief span of history since World War II the international problems confronting our business civilization have seemed numerous and intractable. To make matters worse it has been quite discouraging that out of some solutions have grown new problems.

Consider, for example, our problems vis-à-vis the rest of the world in 1946. At the end of the war it was clear that the power and influence of Europe had declined precipitously. In the past the North Atlantic nations had dominated the world, but they could not control themselves. Japan, the prewar power center of Asia, had been crushed in defeat. China, big if not powerful, was still at war with itself. The United States and Russia emerged as the two dominant powers.

In this environment it was evident to the businessman that those countries with market economies must be restored to vitality. The Communist bloc of nations sought self-sufficiency within itself, and Russia was evidencing growing hostility to the United States. Thus, in spite of the fact that he had a long history of isolationism in his background, the businessman came to support aid to Europe, and even gave generously of his know-how in addition to dollars in an effort to revitalize those states. Japan, too, was encouraged by freely proffered aid to resume its brand of capitalism.

Now, of course, the world is taking different shape. Europe and Japan have been restored to economic health. Out of the restoration of Europe, however, comes a new challenge to the present structure of our business system.

A part of the European response to the predicament into which she had fallen was a joining together of six states into a Common Market. This was a logical consequence of much that had gone before. Germany and France, powerful states only a short time ago, had each been humiliated by defeat during World War II. They could, with this in their immediate past, more easily forget their long enmity and join together. In addition, the physical enormity of the two great powers—the United States and the U.S.S.R.—made it seem a far distant day indeed when a single European state could assume real significance. A jointure seemed a way to telescope time and sooner cast a shadow over the events of the world. Nuclear weapons appeared to render the small nation obsolete. Postage-stamp and somewhat larger nations could readily contemplate their total obliteration. Finally, the dissolution of colonial empires probably improved the climate for the Common Market. With other trading ties dissolving it was easier to form new ones. Of course, these forces helping to forge a union of European nations are all in addition to the solid sense that such an endeavor had always made.

While this new entity was in its primitive and adolescent stages, the United States assumed certain attitudes toward it. At that time, of course, the Common Market was extremely dependent upon this country. It was tempting for us to extrapolate the behavior characteristics of that span out into the future. We did not successfully resist such temptation. Soon United States policy seemed to assume a perpetually friendly relationship with a somewhat subservient union in Europe.

Suddenly, this view of the present and future was shattered. The friendly union in Europe turned, if not hostile, at least competitive. Great Britain was denied membership probably mostly because of long-time friendly associations with the United States. There was a feeling, in France especially, that England would act as instrument for United States policies. American visions of a permanent partnership with Europe were blurred. The European Common Market was a "big boy" now and as such it served notice that it wanted to walk alone.

Now, if England enters it will be only after exhibiting a suitable orthodoxy in attitude. England will not get in as special representative of the United States. This means that her getting in holds less significance to us except that it would still be desirable as providing a measure of political stability and sophistication.

Of course, it is difficult to say just how this switch in world arrangements is affecting the businessman. Like the rest of us, so far he seems reluctant to admit what has happened really did. "Even De Gaulle must die some day, and when he does the Common Market will turn back into what we thought it was," businessmen seem to be saying. He will, but it won't, would probably be a more realistic verdict.

I think, too, that what has occurred will gradually come to be recognized as changing fairly dramatically the world market system. Consider only in barest outline what has happened. Formerly, the United States traded with six economically independent nations no one of which was more than 30 per cent as large in terms of population or physical dimension and comparatively much smaller in total product.

Now a single economic unit of size commensurate with the United States in all but total product has been erected in place of the six. Would the policies and practices of the United States Steel Corporation be influenced if six of its rivals joined together to form a unit of roughly commensurate size if not current earning power? The question is not whether, it is how.

Already it is possible to see dimly what is coming up. In my view it is not exactly what the businessman has been led to expect. It is not being defeatist—merely realistic—to expect that the European union will inhibit the flow of trade from here to there for the rest of this decade, at least.

A lot of work remains to be done in Europe—work that does not really involve the United States; work that might be better accomplished from their standpoint if our intrusions are held to a minimum. A customs union—this is, after all, basically what the Common Market is—logically involves economic union also. Only now through the planned abolishment of the classical barriers to trade among the members, is the Common Market community becoming a full-fledged customs union. The next step, and it is being taken, is to remove other less obvious distortions impeding the unrestricted flow of goods. Then, of course, if goods are to move freely, so also must money and if the result is to be relocation of resources, investment capital and manpower must be liberated too. All these changes tearing down barriers among Common Market nations must naturally make anachronistic separate national policies in many fields—social, political, monetary, and economic.

While all this is taking place there is a good chance that the Common Market community will seek to protect itself.

Overall tariff levels may not rise, but imports will be prevented from destroying the integration of producing units within the union. Even after the period of transition, a real economic partnership between the United States and Europe may have to wait. As long as the United States dwarfs the Common Market community in power and income, real bargaining cannot be accomplished. Can American Motors go into partnership with General Motors? In my view, it cannot. It can merge with General Motors and be swallowed up, but because of the difference in power and wealth a real partnership cannot be formed.

The role that the businessman will play in all of this is difficult to ascertain. Philosophically, he would like to think of himself as a free trader. Actually, he has only been thus when he has had all the advantages his way. Always, he has had the ready excuse that high wages in this country put him at a disadvantage.

Recently it has become quite stylish for American businessmen to use excess funds generated in United States companies to establish overseas affiliates; but if this trend were to continue at the current pace neither the United States nor some of the foreign countries would be too happy. The impact on our balance of payments is unfortunate. Nations for the most part do not welcome widespread ownership of industry by foreign powers.

What United States businessmen, then, must be prepared to face is a long period of ever-increasing competition with the European union. The Common Market is Europe's answer to the challenge of size that faces all modern economies in the present stage of technology. Now for the first time German auto makers and French farmers will have a vast home market for their products. This will make a difference.

It will make a difference to United States producers too. One of our historical advantages is being wiped out. Formerly, we were the only really advanced industrial economy with a large home market for its output. This gave us economies of scale not enjoyed elsewhere.

Quite likely the continued success of the Common Market venture will bring emulation. Already this is happening for defensive reasons, if not out of the motive of imitation. Economic blocs are forming and will form. Within these blocs trade will move more freely—without, however, chance of restriction increases. The United States, too large to join a bloc, may find it increasingly difficult to play the free-trade, free-market game in a world consolidating itself into economically proportionate dimensions.

Business units within this country may be forced into a closer relationship with government in order to secure markets abroad. For a time at least, the level of exports may be determined more by the terms of bilateral agreements between this government and each economic union than by comparative costs and prices in the various markets.

Other forces are at work that might prohibit a rising flow of trade between the Common Market and the United States. Just as the great postwar boom in the United States ended five or six years ago, so, too, the boom in Europe and Japan may be nearing its termination now.

The years of strong inflationary pressure, abundant job opportunities, and easy growth ended for the United States about 1957. Not that the years since have been marked by a sudden reversal of these trends, but the years since have been different. Most essential to this difference has been the fact that scarcity has been replaced by abundance. Capacity is more than ample to supply all the existing and foreseeable needs of American consumers.

Now this same pervasive change is coming over the economies of the rest of the Free World. There is unmistakable evidence that a new stage is being reached in industrialized Europe.

As was the case in this country, the first reaction of our foreign friends seems to be disbelief. There is a certain reluctance on the part of everyone to believe something that is unpleasant. They are finding, however, that price rises are not so easy to pass along, wage rises come at the expense of profits and perhaps jobs, growth is coming a bit harder.

All this will be immensely important to American businessmen. With excess productive capacity in the United States and the European union, reliance on market forces to work out necessary adaptations will be nearly impossible. It would be as if General Motors and Ford slugged it out in the old-fashioned, price-cutting way. Damage would be far reaching. Modern democratic societies will not tolerate such eventualities. Instead, more and more the temptation will be to enter into arrangements that allocate markets. In Europe this process has a long history. Cartels have in the past dominated industry in Europe.

It is going to be difficult to prevent free world economies from slipping back into this old habit. Even here in the United States there is some sentiment for what are, in effect, cartels. Assured markets, steady profits, low break-even points, these are what cartels seek to achieve. It is a pretty heady mixture, but America has shown there is a way between old-fashioned competition and cartels. America must get its economy functioning efficiently again in order that its way has maximum appeal.

If some of the evidence suggests trade with the European union will face numerous new inhibitors in the coming decade, impediments to trade with the Communist bloc of nations may tend to dissolve somewhat. It is always difficult to say what is going on behind the walls. What seems true, however, is that Red rulers are being pressed to give increasingly more output to consumers. That Communists still depend upon intimidation and chimerical crises to maintain their grip on Eastern Europe says a great deal. More and more, urgencies are causing them to "Westernize" their society.

At present the bulk of Russian trade is in raw materials. Currently, the Communists export to the rest of the world something like $5 billion of goods annually. Generally speaking, Communist leaders have gone out of their way to emphasize how little dependent they are on this trade, how well they could get along without it. This attitude is changing somewhat—probably in response to compulsion from within as their society nears Western standards of consumer creature comforts.

Up to now trade between the Communist countries and the West has not brought all the normal incidental advantages of economic contact. There is coming to be, however, reciprocal travel, and limited intermingling of peoples. This is only a bare beginning. Certainly, there is nothing like the kind of relationships that normally evolve from trading among nations with businessmen living in other countries and forming friendships with foreigners.

The Soviet government, by maintaining a monopoly of foreign trade and conducting most of its transactions abroad, pretty much precludes the ancillary benefits from accruing. Nonetheless, the Communist "image" is beginning to change. They seem now to be paying their bills more promptly, trying to impress with their reliability, and they are even showing a good bit of interest in Western advertising and marketing techniques. They are coming to be more businesslike in their dealings.

In spite of these signs, it is hard to believe that trade with Russia and the rest of the Communist bloc will have much impact, beneficial or otherwise, on the American businessman in the near future. Russia and the United States over their histories have never traded much with each other except in time of war. Russian products appear clumsy and dated by Western standards; it is difficult to imagine them "stealing" many markets. The purchasing programs of the Soviet Foreign Trade Monopoly have political as well as economic implications. Non-Communist governments must always be careful lest exchanges built up over years involving important commitments on the part of Western firms may be prematurely ended for reasons other than those economic. This transiency arises from the absence of commercial self-interest on the side of the Soviets, and it places definite limitations on the good that can be expected to flow from the more hopeful signs behind the walls.

On the other hand, Russia and the United States have compatible farm problems. The farm problem there arises out of bad climate and inefficiencies. Here the problem is that we are so efficient. In Russia they have maybe 40 per cent of their labor force producing farm goods and are still not able to satisfy demand. In this country we produce much more than we need with about one-fourth of their percentage.

It seems natural, therefore, for our two countries to get together and trade. A lot will depend on actions by both sides surrounding the proposed grain sales to the Soviet bloc. If mutually profitable trade develops, it could be the start of something big. That the businessman will be wary goes without saying. So will the Russians. Both nations would have a lot of words to swallow before a real trading partnership develops. The Russians have shown how fast they can change their tune repeatedly (remember when Joseph Stalin was a hero); and the American businessman is schizophrenic. It is a long shot to be sure, but possibly trade with the Soviet bloc will increase quite perceptibly over the next decade.

What is important insofar as the Communists are concerned is that the Western world has come to put them in new perspective over the past few years. Clearly, their system holds out few temptations for advanced civilizations. Even the Reds are coming to comprehend and increasingly admit that they have more to learn from us than vice versa. The danger to America is that, more out of habit than anything else, businessmen and the rest of us will continue to be preoccupied with Red rumblings. Their society will have many more adjustments forced on it by us than it can efficiently handle over the next decade. It would be well if we gave them little attention until they digest some of this. They are not nearly the menace to us that we are to them. Our faith that in the long contest the Communists will be converted to our way of thinking rather than we to theirs is completely justified. After nearly 20 years of Communism, Russia would not be willing to risk any sort of free election in East Germany or Eastern Europe, and she herself is taking first steps toward Westernization.

It is especially important that we maintain cool perspective so that proportionate attention can be devoted to the so-called "poor" nations of the world. The average annual income in the United States is probably more than twenty times that of a third of the world's population. A number of fine books have been written to tell us of this and, perhaps even more important, to make us aware that the rich nations are getting richer and the poor poorer. This tendency is not easy to reverse. Barbara Ward has observed: "It is very much easier for a rich man to invest and grow richer than for the poor man to begin investing at all. And this is also true of nations."

Unhappily, we have discovered that there is a vast difference between restoring to business health the war-devastated economies of Europe and aiding the impoverished former colonies of the world. Europe had the roughly appropriate habits, institutions, and attitudes necessary for a modern industrial civilization. All the nations there needed was material help toward revitalization. The essential problem in the poor nations of the world is not of the same stripe. Material wealth seems wasted on them. They have not developed the kinds of civilizations that know how to utilize capital to become industrial societies.

To put it mildly, the businessman feels frustrated by all this. It is to his eternal credit that he does not revert to stereotype and reassume his isolationist stance. Somehow he rightly senses it is too late for that. But what can he do?

His instincts tell him that you get what you deserve. If

some nations are rich and others poor, it is because the rich are much better at the economic game than the poor. What can you do about that? What would you want to do?

Instinctively, then, the businessman does not want to do anything about this eventuality of the economic game. But just as he has come to understand that in a modern industrial nation the harsh consequences of the free enterprise game must be softened, so has he come to realize that the world order demands similar modifications in favor of the weak. This is especially the case when, as at present, the United States enjoys a living standard even beyond what most of the rest of the world considers luxurious.

But giving money or goods to these nations does not seem to be the answer. If by such actions our business society succeeds in lifting living standards somewhat in a poor nation, it usually proves temporary. Population gains and other adjustments occur and wipe out the advance. How can you make a nation grow and prosper if by its actions it proves it does not so desire?

Of course, the answer that the businessman gets to this question is that these countries have the desire, they just do not know how. The kind of know-how they need is not easily imported in the face of centuries of bad habits by the standards of an industrial society.

Perhaps, the most important contribution the American businessman can make to the poorer third of the world is negative. In the face of great temptation to the contrary he can refrain from trying to impose his values on these nations. Many of these states are trying to race into the 1960s. With modern societies all about them they are not willing to build an industrial complex as the West did, by stages from handicraft to automation. They want it all at once, and now. They want giant steel mills, although they have never successfully operated small ones; they want automobiles, but they don't have highways; and they want modern factories, yet they don't know what to produce. They do not understand that they have to pay a price to successfully industrialize a nation. Over the course of the next few years they are going to learn this lesson. It is my guess that, as they understand some of what is involved, certain of them will decide they do not want a modern economy enough to pay for it.

Strong leaders, however, will try to "force" industrialization on them. Robert L. Heilbroner said in his book *The Great Ascent:* "The price of development is apt to be political and economic authoritarianism. . . . Strongman governments and collectivist economic techniques are apt to be the accompaniments of development in backward areas—not as mere excrescences of, but as necessary conditions for, an effort great enough to sustain the enormous process."

Necessary or not this is not a prescription apt to find approval within the business community. For the businessman to give aid to nations characterized by political dictatorship and economic collectivism will take some doing. Of course, he has done it in the recent past, but now the price is higher. Not necessarily in direct charges, but as reflected through the outflow of gold. It was fairly easy to be generous when inflation was fuzzing analysis of just what was occurring. Vision is now clear. America is sacrificing growth at home to send funds abroad.[1]

---

[1] At first glance there will be many who would dispute this statement. The point is that the United States is not able to pursue expansionary domestic policies because of the balance of payments problem.

Only as the businessman is reminded and convinced of the necessity for these funds will he continue to go along with such payments. He will need to be assured that the nations receiving aid are doing all they can for themselves. He will want to know if they are taking appropriate steps to raise food productivity in order to free labor for industrial jobs. Are social attitudes changing in a way conducive to building a modern industrial society? Are the jobs that can be accomplished by peasant labor without sophisticated capital equipment in process? If these conditions are met, chances are strong that except in the case of lands headed by professional anti-Americans, aid will be given without opposition from the business community. The businessman understands that many kinds of tools and apparatus are impossible to produce in underdeveloped regions. Much machinery requires prior machinery. Trucks, lathes, and machine shops can't be constructed by the eagerest workers equipped only with primitive tools.

If his conditions to be met for the giving of aid sound "tough" to some, they seem realistic to me. Even now there is coming to be a consensus among foreign aid professionals that in the future more selectivity is in order. My guess is that less money will be wasted if the business community influences government to use its standards of choice.

The real danger for the future from underdeveloped areas would arise in the event that America acquires a reputation for backing existing regimes no matter how incapable they might be. It is not in our best tradition to ferment foreign revolutions, but at least we can show discrimination in the dispensing of funds.

The United States has a bad reputation in South America

in particular, as a result of seeming to support corrupt re-gimes so long as "Yankee" business interests are protected. If the businessman has helped to mislead our government along this shortsighted path in the past, he should not in the future. The businessman's interests have broadened. His cause won't be helped by protecting business interests if the price of such protection involves the propping-up of govern-ments inimical to the interests of the affected nation.

Neither should the businessman insist that aid be given to only those nations developing along capitalistic lines. Among the various poor nations of the world each has its own peculi-arities, its own set of values. It is impossible for the United States to prescribe the precise measures suitable for develop-ment in these nations. What happened here may not have application there.

In the early days of this nation, industrialists were free to pay low wages and to secure high profits. Taxes were low, almost nonexistent. These arrangements provided great in-centive to businessmen.

Today, attitudes developed in the mature rich countries are generally adopted by the poor. Labor unions demand high wages, squeezing profits. Taxes are heavy on what remains. Thus, the free enterprise process of industrialization in the poor countries tends to be sluggish. Prospective business leaders are discouraged by dim profit potentialities. The temptation for the state to assume more responsibility for business development becomes nearly irresistible.

Of course, the American businessman would like social attitudes within the poor countries to change. To him it is perfectly obvious that economic factors are of relatively small consequence. He would hope that by imposing capitalism on the poor nations he would alter the actions of people in a way commensurate with economic growth and well-being. It seems instead, that the people of these lands alter capitalism in a way that inhibits growth and maintains living standards at depressed levels.

Adding everything together, predictable events in the rest of the world would not seem too upsetting for the American business community. True enough, the Common Market throws a real challenge at us. Adjustments on both sides of the Atlantic will have to come. On the whole, however, the free societies of the world should gain in strength as a result. Communism seems not so threatening to our way of life as formerly imagined; in fact, there is some tendency for a Westernization in parts of the Red world. The problem here may be to put the Communists in new perspective and not let their boasting and truculence divert us from more vexing problems. The underdeveloped lands will probably frustrate efforts to enrich them perceptibly. Perhaps the "tough" conditions of the businessman will work better than the more "charitable" approach of some of his contemporaries. In any event, he can no longer afford to promote policies designed to protect his narrow interests.

14

Automation: Less Need for Profits?

In the year 1810, English weavers smashed textile machines, burned factories, and assaulted businessmen in a vain attempt to prevent the extinction of their trade. Within 50 years the weaving occupation as performed in 1810 had all but vanished. A skill had been wiped out. Holders of this skill had to adjust their lives to the new realities. The price of progress was paid by a relatively small group of displaced workers.

Of course, by 1860 employment in the textile industry in England was well beyond the level employed 50 years earlier and output was many times what it had been.

Since that time the preceding experience in one form or another has repeated itself over and over again. Gradually, however, the price paid for technological progress has been shared more widely. Now the Maximum Employment Act of 1946—popularly known as the full employment act —implicitly promises each person in the work force that he will get a job or receive income while temporarily not working. What this means is that the rules of the economic game have become such that the laid-off workers stay in our business system's overall cost figures whether or not they find reemployment. In a few cases strong unions have even forced employers to maintain workers in obsolete occupations—featherbedding—until retirement or other form of voluntary separation ended their working lives.

In 1810 all but a very few lived rather wretchedly by present standards. Men, women, and children worked from sunup to sundown six days a week in unsanitary, unsafe, virtually unbearable surroundings. Pay was kept at a subsistence level and jobs were nearly always hard to find. The overwhelming majority of the people in each nation was barely able to keep itself alive. No matter how income and the fruits of production had been distributed there would not have been enough for a decent standard of living for all. Within this environment those introducing sharply more productive, laborsaving machines and techniques could easily convince themselves and most others that, despite short-run dislocations, the advances they were sponsoring were necessary for the long-run benefit of society and the survival of the business system.

Since that time conditions of life in the United States especially have changed dramatically. A 40-hour workweek is standard. Coffee breaks, piped-in music, and noise modulation make pleasant the working environment. Take-home pay enables the average worker to subsist in a six-room house equipped with automobile, television set, refrigerator, and other appliances. The overwhelming majority of the population seems reasonably satisfied with its standard of life. Given the appropriate distribution of income, more than enough productive capacity exists to produce a good standard of living for all. These conditions alter appreciably the environment within which sharply more productive, laborsaving machines and techniques are introduced. There seems much less certainty today that such changes are necessary for the long-run benefit of society and survival of the business system.

Despite the sharply changed environment—the full employment philosophy, and the level of affluence—so accustomed have Americans become to change that there would probably be little question about the necessity of utilizing additional work-saving equipment were it not for a word. The word, of course, is automation.

It is a characteristic of modern society in America that "tags" or "labels" are important. Dwight D. Eisenhower would have been elected without it, but the "Ike" label helped his popularity. Conversely, calling Richard M. Nixon "Tricky Dick" could have cost him the Presidency. No self-respecting writer has called a conference of the heads of states anything but "summit conference" for a few years now. Some say if the Edsel had been named anything but that, it would still be on the market. Certainly, it seems true that "automation" would not assume quite such awesome proportions were it called technological innovation or almost anything else.

True enough, certain distinctions might be made between the changes called automation and other technological advances. It is alleged that up until now capital equipment has basically and spectacularly augmented man's muscle power. Now what is called automation replaces his hands, fingers, nose, eyes, ears, and brain. It is one thing to help man by extinguishing the need for hard labor, it is quite another to replace him in pleasanter occupations.

To the businessman, this is a rather meaningless distinction. Machines have been displacing workers in the short run and adding to production and employment in the long run for some time. If in the current fashion different occupations or skills are being affected, it was ever thus. Certainly, there is little real distinction between the replacement of a worker doing a routine job in a factory and one punching an adding machine in an office.

I know a number of business leaders who laugh at the notion that computers are replacing office workers. "Computers are making it too easy to keep mountains of unnecessary detail," a president of a medium-sized factory in Cheshire, Connecticut, told me. His point was that more savings by far would come from eliminating much of the minutia computers compile than from trying to make sense from all the numbers now collected and more. In other words, computers won't replace office workers because they will spin off more needless information requiring more people to comprehend.

Certainly, there is no convincing evidence to substantiate the notion that since the introduction of automation there has been a noticeable surge in productivity. In fact the productivity of production workers in manufacturing rose much faster in the 1920's than since 1948. In the recent period the farm sector, where no one calls what is taking place automation, shows the most rapid advance in productive efficiency.

It is interesting that in 1927 the Secretary of Labor's report to Congress observed: "One of the more serious aspects [of unemployment] is in the tendency of laborsaving machinery to displace hand workers at a rate more rapid than they can be absorbed in new pursuits. We must guard against the general economic loss we shall suffer if laborsaving machinery is to load us down with chronic increases in the nonproductive and unemployed."

To the businessman historical items such as this put into proper perspective what is taking place today. Social and economic problems surrounding automation have not suddenly sprung to life. In the broadest sense, automation represents merely the latest step in the evolution of technology.

Louis G. Seaton of General Motors points out that: "Contrary to popular impression, mechanization—or automation—has not reduced the number of man-hours that go into building a General Motors automobile. The reason is that the greatly improved cars and trucks of today are mechanically more complex and hence more complicated to produce than their counterparts of even a few years ago. . . . Accordingly, the number of cars produced per employee per year has remained substantially constant over the years."

The business view of the furor over automation could be summarized by the following paragraph.

Each year since such things began being measured, the American economy has been able to produce as much as in the year preceding, with fewer workers. Recently, the normal improvement in efficiency has supplanted 1.5 to 2 million workers each year. As long as total spending increases fast enough to accommodate the otherwise displaced and the net additions to the work force, little concern and much approbation are expressed over the technological advances. When, however, demand increases slowly as for the past six years or so, increasing attention is centered on laborsaving machinery as a cause of unemployment. The word "automation" magnifies this concern.

But if the businessman is not alarmed about automation, others are. Norbert Wiener, of the Massachusetts Institute of Technology, in discussing the new automated machines has said: "This new revolution will produce an unemployment situation in comparison with which . . . the depression of the 1930s will seem a pleasant joke." The 1962 television show "Automation: The Awesome Servant" and the pamphlet "Cybernation: The Silent Conquest" served to enlarge apprehension.

Businessmen, though predominantly of the view described before, are not completely immune to the spreading concern over automation. Thomas J. Watson, Jr., Chairman of International Business Machines Corporation, told the House Automation Subcommittee in mid-1961: "We seem to have automated our country sufficiently to supply all the basic demands and a good many luxuries, and still involve only 93 per cent of our work force. . . . If all the things which need to be done are worked into a national plan and begun in the near future, we can turn unemployment into an employment shortage and at the same time make our country so strong that we will create a much greater deterrence from attack than we have today."

My own view is closer to the dominant business position on automation. I am persuaded that the unemployment of the past few years is mostly the result of the filling of war-induced shortages, changes in the "mix" of demand, and the reemergence of foreign competition. Unquestionably, automation has augmented unemployment within this climate. It is difficult to ascertain how much. In most cases where automation is alleged to have caused distress, other reasons fuzz up perspective. For example, important changes in the market for cars occurred just at the time Detroit really began automating.

Changes growing out of technological innovations have always been notoriously difficult to measure, and are almost always much broader than imagined. The automobile, for example, did infinitely more than just supplant the buggy. It mainly replaced staying at home, and is now transplanting cities, towns, and the whole countryside. Now, automation may be replacing certain skills; but more important, it is transforming our educational needs. In this statement I do not mean to suggest that we shall have to train workers to man the new automated equipment. Computers and other forms of automated equipment are giant morons not giant brains. Even the highly regarded "programming" of a computer is difficult not because of the inherent complexity of the computer itself, but because of the need to spell out every minute step in painstaking detail. Just as most of the jobs replaced by the computer did not call for highly intelligent or creative people, neither does most work with the computer. On the other hand, the incessant load of information emptying from the computer begs for more general intelligence in its use and interpretation. A more theoretical bent in education as opposed to our traditional pragmatic bias in this country would seem appropriate if we are to take full advantage of automation.

Despite my relative complacency concerning that which is

called automation, I do think it is helping to bring certain
changes which threaten, to some extent, the well-being of our
economy. This is even more the case because these changes
are going largely unrecognized.

At the present time it is quite possible that a structural
change is taking place in the role which private capital—plant and equipment—plays in our economy. All of the
talk about automation over the past decade or so would
suggest that spending for new plant, and especially machinery, has been tremendous. Actually, it has been anything but.
The short fall in plant and equipment spending has been
obscured by the magnitude of the raw figures. They have
been impressive.

The failure of investment in plant and machinery is not a
failure to grow, but a failure to grow enough to hold its
proportionate part of GNP. There is a persuasive enough
explanation for this. After the shortage-induced postwar
boom in capital investment a letdown was inevitable. Every
capital spending boom is bound to bring in its wake some
excess capacity. In fact, the astonishing part is not that there
has been a letdown, rather that the letdown has been so
gentle, unlike what happened subsequent to the capital
investment boom of the twenties.

Obviously, in part at least, I subscribe to the foregoing
explanation. Some of what has been said in preceding chapters shows that. Nonetheless, an important part of the story
remains untold. The amount of capital—plant and equipment—required per dollar of output, call it the capital-output ratio, has been declining. This ratio has decreased considerably since the 1920s. The Council of Economic Advisers
has estimated that this ratio dropped from 2.3 (i.e., $2.30 of

capital to $1 of output) in 1929, when the series begins, to
about 1.8 in the period since the war. That is more than a 20
per cent decline.

Other bits of evidence, to be sure difficult to validate, suggest that the capital-output ratio has been falling fairly consistently since 1900. Without delving further into the statistics
surrounding the notion, it is enough to say that what all of
this implies is that quite possibly the American economy has
reached the stage where technological development is so
productive that less is needed. In other words, the normal
increase in productivity per man-hour will come from a
lesser increase in capital.

If this is true, and if the need for private capital continues
to decline in relative importance, its eventual impact on the
economy can hardly be exaggerated.

What seems to be happening is that in an evolutionary way
scientific processes—not just automation—are bringing the
American economy to a point where obviously smaller inputs
of capital are producing larger outputs of consumables. In
order for a relatively free-market economy to adjust to this
structural change, consumption expenditures must grow proportionally larger as compared with saving. In the absence of
a steady stream of really exciting new products, there is little
chance of this "just happening" in coincidence with the need
for it. For a time, perhaps, the excessiveness of saving is disguised, as funds chase each other in the stock market, and
find outlet overseas. But if consumer spending stays at the
same percentage of income, saving remains redundant and
business activity is sluggish. In this situation, modern government moves in. Government spending in ever increasing
doses is prescribed. After a time, however, it becomes ob-

vious that government spending is growing larger absolutely and proportionately. Businessmen, in particular, become alarmed and other antidotes are sought.

Unfortunately, it is particularly difficult for businessmen to see this problem in true perspective. First, they can scarcely admit to themselves the need for ever larger government spending, and conversely smaller inputs of capital. Increased reliance on government spending seems to have the many disadvantages discussed in other chapters. Instead, they ask for larger profits, greater permissible allowances for depreciation reserves, and the like so they can hike capital spending back to its former role in the economy. But their own efficiency and inventiveness prevent them from getting it there. It is a paradox not yet sufficiently comprehended that the very productiveness of capital is, in the spending sense, leading to its diminishing role.

Were he to admit to himself that what is outlined here is really happening, what should be the policy of the businessman? Should he sit back and watch government spending grow absolutely and proportionally to compensate for the ever-increasing excess of savings over investment needs? I think not. Without being ridiculously conservative about this, I am still persuaded that ever-increasing reliance on government weakens a society. But I think, too, that misguided efforts to secure tax laws and the like that will restore capital spending to its historic role in the American economy can badly distort our business system. Already, the sought-after and won ability of business to finance itself largely from the internal flow of funds, such as depreciation and undistributed profits, restricts the flow of capital between industries, and has helped produce much idle capacity.

Rather, it seems, business should be for measures that would increase consumption at the expense of saving. I say this appreciating the difficulties of accomplishment. The schizophrenic businessman incessantly advertises to beguile the consumer into buying his product, but has never identified himself with programs to raise overall spending at the expense of saving. This ambiguity has deep roots, partially explained in earlier sections of this book, and will not be easily overcome.

Of course, there are measures that might be expected to increase spending at the expense of saving. One of these involves changes in tax rates. A steeply progressive income tax to redistribute income from the wealthy toward the poor can reasonably be expected to increase spending. There are two fairly strong arguments against this. It has already been used rather extensively, thereby minimizing potential benefits from further income equalization. Perhaps most important, any increase in "progressiveness" might have most unfortunate side effects. Incentives are blunted as taxes near what high earners consider to be confiscatory levels. Already some in our society seem discouraged by tax rates. To incline the rate more steeply would not seem wise in spite of the fact that it could be expected to raise consumer spending proportionately.

The trend toward security is working in favor of spending increases. Job and income insecurity make prudent rather large savings, even for low income receivers. Conversely, the partially successful quest for security has raised spending to a larger proportion of income than would otherwise have been the case. If in the future more workers move from a wage to salary basis—advocated earlier for other reasons—it would enhance the feeling of security, and increase spending at the expense of saving.

Dollars going for research and development might mean more consumer spending. A steady stream of new civilian products is much to be desired. Nothing gives more momentum to spending than an exciting new product. Time was that competitive pressure seemed to squeeze new products out of our business system without a cent being spent directly on research and development. Times have changed. Competition is not the same. Now huge companies set aside equipment, space, and personnel to work adventurously on things new. Unfortunately, as mentioned earlier, military and space requirements have caused government needs to dominate research. Civilian needs have suffered.

As unlikely as it may sound, a major change in advertising emphasis could be helpful. Protestations to the contrary, advertising has changed very little, except in technique, from what it was in its infancy. By now, not much is expected of it. At its most effective it is "gimmicky." At its worst it is an insult to the intelligence of ungifted children. Even so-called "institutional advertising" is usually a thinly disguised recital of the necessity for high profits.

From the preceding I do not intend to give the impression that I am calling for educational advertising. Nothing would be duller than a steady diet of objective, thorough, educational ads. What is needed, I believe, is advertisements with broader perspective. Advertisements that would have as their goal the widening of living-horizons for Americans. Advertising programs that would be put together to show Americans the way toward more enjoyable, worthwhile living.

It would be difficult to accomplish this kind of advertising within the present institutional arrangements. Individual companies want identification for their products to increase company sales. What I am asking is advertising to lift consumers' sights. Individual company sponsorship would prejudice the goals narrowly and defeat the purpose.

Mass business support—financial and psychological— would be required. Even more important, divorcement from sponsor pressure would have to be secured for the advertising agency involved. Perhaps, the agency handling such an assignment would work on no other. The best marketing, economic, and advertising minds in the country would be called together for such a venture. It could evolve into the American answer to government planning.

Finally, and perhaps most important, the corporate profits tax must be eliminated so that total profits of corporations can be reduced. Many industries have a relatively inflexible demand for their products. In other words, sales are not dramatically affected by changes in price within certain limits. Also some of these industries are dominated by firms with the power to administer prices. Although the case is not black and white, it is very probably true that given these circumstances firms will pass along the incidence of the corporate profits tax to the consumer in the form of a higher price. Such action restricts demand.

There are those economists who grant the theoretical sense of corporate profits tax elimination, but aver that removal would not result in lower prices. In their view, firms would maintain present price policies and pocket the share now going to the government. I think they are wrong. The businessman does not admit it openly, but he is aware of the broad changes that have taken place in the American economy.

Truly, our business society realizes it is unrealistic to expect profits to be as high as in decades past. Formerly, high profits were needed to lure cash from current consumption into necessary investment in productive facilities. Now more current consumption is in order. Formerly, high profits seemed only just compensation for the tremendous risks undertaken. Financial panic could bring on depression and ruin the soundest corporation. Now depressions are "against the law," and even recessions do not always check yearly advances in GNP. In this changed environment are high profits really necessary to finance proportionally less investment? Formerly, corporations did not generate as much of their investment funds internally. They had to show good profits to get needed money for expansion. Now huge depreciation allowances and the like permit corporations to "roll their own." It is clear to sophisticated businessmen that profits up to former standards are inappropriate to the times.

What all this seems to mean is that business can adjust to the structural change that a steady stream of scientific developments—including automation—is foisting onto our economy. To adjust, however, businessmen will have to change some of their long-cherished biases. In fact, even if not so voiced, businessmen will have to promote policies that will raise consumer spending at the expense of saving, give employees even more security, and accept as normal a somewhat smaller return as profit. Government will have to have the political courage to eliminate the corporate profits tax.

This tax is not what it seems to be. It has caused higher prices and indirectly influenced corporate policies in a way that results in larger savings. Corporations, seeing half of their profits taken by government, and not sure they can pass the tax on to consumers, probably are led to put emphasis on larger depreciation allowances. To the unsophisticated, however, elimination will seem to be a gift to the businessman.

That this will take some doing goes without saying. If society does not go along with something like this prescription, it is possible that government spending as a proportion of total spending will continue to rise.

15

Affluence and Reasonable Featherbedding

This book began by pointing out that a big change has come over our economic system. The invisible hand of competition, which enabled businessmen to follow their selfish instincts while ensuring that common good would result, is dominant no longer. The businessman, however, is reluctant to openly acknowledge this fact of mid-twentieth-century life. Instead he talks as if what once was still is. This is not particularly harmful—in fact does some good—except when he gets carried away by his own rhetoric and behaves that way too.

Not too long ago John Kenneth Galbraith pointed out another big change, in his view, transforming our business system. *The Affluent Society* says a lot of things. Basically, however, Professor Galbraith points out that the problem of scarcity has been overcome, in the United States at least. This is tremendously important because the American economic system sets out to solve the problem of scarce resources and unlimited desires. The "conventional wisdom" is based on a problem that no longer exists, according to Galbraith. Businessmen will be just as happy if society does not get carried away by Galbraith's rhetoric, and begin behaving as if what he says is true really is.

It is a fitting final paradox for this book, which to some extent has featured business schizophrenia, that businessmen should be concerned that they have achieved what every business system sets out to accomplish.

Certainly, it seems a cruel twist of fate that the very scarcity and poverty that the American business system has wiped out removes its best justification. That by working so well and bringing wealth and affluence, business has produced an environment within which its permanent alteration can reasonably be contemplated may even be made more likely. If redundance has replaced scarcity why worry about the most productive allocation of resources, efficiency, cost-cutting, and so forth? Why be governed by the so-called basic principles and laws of economics?

Now when businessmen ask Americans to accept discipline, to work hard, and to eschew the easy life, most nod assent. But a growing number ask why? Is it really worthwhile for the American economy to grow faster, or to grow much at all? Galbraith does not think so. In fact, he believes that we have reached a point in our economic history at which the striving for ever more production actually creates problems instead of solving them.

Even the idea of growth to beat Russia is derided by Galbraith. The next war probably would be over so fast that only what was produced before it started would be of decisive consequence. Presumably, Russia and the United States have all the needed bombs right now. Each can "overkill" the other.

There is no real sense in producing more so that we can give it away, either. Prosperity in Europe makes it unnecessary for increased production here to subsidize living standards there to gain friends and acquire allies. The difficulty of exporting high standards of life elsewhere is giving reason to wonder about producing more to give more to the underprivileged areas of the world. Much of the aid already provided to the undeveloped areas seems to have had a debilitating effect on the supposed beneficiaries.

Business, then, finds itself in danger of being moved from the center of the stage by the very abundance it has brought into being. The life or death aspects of its struggle seem over, and, there is no question about it, some of the fun is gone.

True enough the Galbraith view is not dominant—is not the conventional wisdom—as yet. Nonetheless, the businessman recognizes that some of what he says rings true. For example, the unemployment that exists does not seem easily amenable to cure by increasing demand, and demand does not seem easy to increase. Other economic problems do not seem so crucial when everyone lives so well. And surely, the game is not the same when the possibility of depression has been eliminated.

What the businesssman firmly believes, however, is that if the principles that have brought success are abandoned, then plenty will quickly disappear and scarcity return. In other words, we have to keep playing the game, if for fun, so that its life-or-death aspects don't reappear.

The businessman can easily convince himself of this. But can he convince others, or how can he convince others? First, let it be admitted that he must recognize that affluence cannot be ignored. A *Business Week* editorial in April, 1963, pointed out: "If the long strike-lockout involving New York newspapers proved anything it was this: In an affluent society, the strike ceases to be an effective way of settling an issue between powerful employers and equally powerful unions. The resources of both sides are so great that there is no compelling pressure upon them to bargain in dead earnest. For weeks and months, the principal sufferer is the general public rather than any of the parties directly involved."

Strikes are far from the only institutions rendered anachronistic by affluence. Some alterations must be forthcoming.

Our present economic beliefs and pattern of institutional arrangements came into being when the most urgent need of any business system was defined in terms of an increase in production. Today we have large-scale agricultural surpluses and, with existing facilities, the ability to produce $60 billion worth of goods and services beyond that which is being demanded. Slowly, Americans are coming to realize that available resources could be used to abolish poverty, if we could only find a way to liberate resources for this purpose without destroying the kind and quality of life desired.

It is up to the businessman to find such a means. If he does not, others in our society will not be so patient or so concerned about potential consequences. As the level of potential abundance comes to be commonly recognized and if the gap between actual output and capacity production widens, there will come to be increasing pressure to divide things up on a more or less giveaway basis. Then the game the businessman loves, and which brought affluence to the world in the first place, will be lost.

Predictably, the businessman, to some extent at least, reacts to the challenge of affluence by pretending that it does not exist. Business has good reason for this response. Haste in acting on that which is only dimly perceived is not wise. However, the price of postponement is rising, and becoming more apparent. Even now he is beginning to publicly acknowledge what he has subconsciously perceived for some time. He avers that the present structure of the economy makes it difficult to come to full employment. But what he is prescribing as a cure is from an old book that only he now reads, and in fact even he no longer believes as before.

In June, 1963, Martin Gainsbrugh, chief economist, National Industrial Conference Board, gave voice to the traditional business response in a panel session before the National Association of Purchasing Agents. Dr. Gainsbrugh is a brilliant economist, and through his position eloquently speaks for the businessman.

Someone made the point at this session that a burst of consumer spending would be necessary to bring the economy to a position of full employment. Everyone including Dr. Gainsbrugh agreed. Later, however, a questioner asked if tax relief would be a wise policy to restore health to the economy. Dr. Gainsbrugh said yes, if it is the right type. It turned out that he thought the right type was a reduction in the corporate tax rate and further liberalization in depreciation allowances.

As a member of the panel, I could not help but point out that there seemed to have been general assent to an increase in consumer spending as desirable. Why then, I asked, should the emphasis in tax relief be on investment income? The answer was that of course that was true but was, after all, "putting the cart before the horse." Investment spending to create new jobs was the first step.

It is really rather astonishing the way the business community of recent years has discussed under one heading the unfortunate fact of existing excess capacity, and then under another heading has called for higher levels of investment activity, as though the cure for excess capacity were more capacity.

Robert S. Schultz, director of statistical analysis for the Union Bag-Camp Paper Corporation of New York, wrote in the *Harvard Business Review* in the summer of 1963 that: "Sometimes one feels as if he is the only sane person in a lunatic asylum. . . . I attended a meeting on the business outlook where various leading industrialists discussed the prospects for their particular industries. Invariably, each man said in effect, 'Things in my industry are pretty bad; prices are low because there is too much capacity; and we need to get our prices up so that we can make more profits in order to pay for more capacity expansion.' And as each industrialist concluded this preposterous threnody of circular illogic, he was warmly applauded by his listeners. . . ."

The businessman will stick with his fundamentals: You must have saving before you have investment; somebody has to invest to give someone else a job; a job is required before there can be income; and income is needed for spending. His story is logical, appealing, and easy to understand.

It has never gone unchallenged. Abundance or affluence, whichever you choose to call it, provides new ammunition for the challengers. They start from the assumption that we have now or will have in the very near future a productive system of virtually unlimited capacity. A productive abundance that will far outrun our capacity to consume within traditional income-earning arrangements.

Robert Theobald, an economist and author, has observed: "We are trapped by 'the dismal science'—economics. The founders of economic theory believed that we could *never* achieve abundance and therefore defined economics as the art of 'distributing scarce resources'. . . . The Era of Abundance has arrived. . . . The reverse side of an economy of abundance is the fact that a large proportion of the population will have to be provided with resources even if they are not carrying out a conventional market job—a shocking thought to many, who will be quick to label any such plan as *The Great Giveaway,* or maybe *The Lifelong Vacation Guide.* . . . Financial incentives and inducements will play a limited role in the socioeconomic system of the future."

What this is saying, of course, is that there will not be enough spending to consume all that we are capable of producing unless we give money away. While at this time this may seem a rather wild notion, it is altogether possible that events will conspire in such a way as to make it seem more and more like a plausible solution to the problems involved in an economy dominated by affluence. Over the past 30 years or so there has come to America an implicit belief that government has some sort of responsibility for providing each person with the bare necessities of life. It is not such a long step to the point where government is assumed to have responsibility for giving each person a standard of living to which he would like to become accustomed, or at least to which he has at some time past accustomed himself.

Certainly, it is not difficult to visualize a situation within which it would seem easier for the government to keep the economy rolling with larger handouts for not working rather than to provide jobs for all those who want them. W. H. Ferry has said on this subject: "Abundance may compel social justice as conscience never has. The liberated margin (the unemployed) will have to get 'what is its due.' This means developing a basis of distribution of income which is not tied to work as a measure. For decisions about 'due-ness' will have to be made without economic criteria; at least without the criterion of what members of the liberated margin are worth in the employment market, for there is no such market for them."

Such a general plan will not stumble over the question of how much to give. Once the idea of income without work is established, the problem of how much is tackled. Robert Theobald has recommended that payments be based on committed spending. "Government payments under Committed Spending would be related to the recipients' former incomes. These higher payments, compared to those available under Basic Economic Security, would allow members of this middle-class group to continue the expenditures to which they had become committed by their way of life, and which are vital to the short-run stability of the country."

Financing the giving of money would involve increases in government debt each year. This too, may seem a long step to some of us, but is really not too far removed from what is conceivable.

It would not startle anyone if I predict that neither the traditional business response nor the Theobald approach will be the solution to the challenge of abundance. First, I would say that the very concept of abundance is open to question. It is true that at this time our business system is able to produce more than we seem to want to consume, but there are maybe 10 to 20 per cent of us living below what would seem to be an appropriate American standard of life. Of course, theoretically these are the persons to whom Dr. Theobald and others would give a higher standard of life; these are the persons who would find jobs if more funds were invested in new plant and machinery, according to Dr. Gainsbrugh.

Actually, however, to give them money for a higher standard of life would seem to run the risk of destroying the essence of our business system. It would be nice if each of us would do his best job where most needed whether or not he was rewarded for it, or whether or not he had to in order to receive a certain income. It would be nice, but we will not. If the person who does not work is rewarded as amply or more so than the jobholder, it destroys our kind of business system. More important, it flies in the face of what we have come to consider "fair." To the idealist this is ridiculous. He says, what about the very rich, who need not work; what about the pensioner, and so forth. The answer is that in our society it seems reasonable that the very rich shouldn't have to work (although most of them do something to be "respectable"), and that the pensioner should receive income is part of the bargain he made with his employer. Somewhat more reluctantly we have come to conclude that the unemployed should be supported, but not so adequately as those working. To give away a higher standard of life for not working than is being received by many who work would not seem reasonable, would be deeply resented, and would undermine the foundation of our business system.

I am equally skeptical about the solution offered by the businessman to bring the economy up to capacity operation and the 10 or 20 per cent of the population to adequately higher standards of life. Scarcity and abundance are relative concepts. I do not want to make a black and white case for either. Nonetheless, I think that, on balance, the American economic system is threatened more by abundance than scarcity. Strenuous efforts to promote saving to enable investment are most appropriate when the dominant problem is scarce resources spread thinly in an effort to satisfy excessive demand. In this environment someone must abstain from purchasing consumable goods in the short run in order that factories may be constructed to increase output in the long run.

When abundance is the problem, increased saving cuts back needed current consumption in the short run in an effort to increase production in the long run. All of which would seem to perpetuate the problem. The problem is made to seem more complex by those who argue that investment is needed to get new, more efficient machines to lower costs to meet foreign competition. Of course, the short-run impact of such a policy is to raise costs. In the United States, exports have exceeded imports by over 30 per cent for the past few years. Even at that, certain industries might require special help to be competitive in the long run. It is immeasurably more efficient to build a higher tariff wall around them rather than to undertake policies that will raise saving and investment so high as to cause some to spill over into these less favored industries.

What is needed, rather than either prescription mentioned, is a desire by Americans for a significantly higher standard of life, and an increase in their purchasing power to enable them to realize the new goals. Each of these necessities could come to pass.

We could indeed be fast approaching the day when Americans will lift their sights and "desire" themselves up to a new plane of material life, a new significantly faster rate of economic growth, and on the way use up the abundance there is said to be.

A generation of new adults is fast coming on us. Now and over the next few years the first human products of the postwar period are reaching maturity—becoming full-fledged adults with all the prerogatives that the attainment of this station of life normally confers. For the first time adults whose entire environmental conditioning has come in the years since World War II are upon us.

The sheer size of this group insures that it will have a dramatic impact on our society. Immediately following World War II the birthrate soared. As a consequence, now the number of teenagers is zooming and the number of young adults is following suit. In 1962 about 3,200,000 Americans reached 18 years of age. This is 50 per cent more than in earlier postwar years. By 1970 the number of people in the 18 to 21 age group will be one and a half times as great as in 1955.

It is not just quantity, however, that will distinguish the new adults. They will be different qualitatively as well. Of course, the future is a continuation of the past and those reaching adulthood in the near future will be much like those who reached this stage in the 1950s, the 1940s, the 1930s, and, yes, even the 1920s and before. After all, these are their parents and grandparents.

But there will be differences. The years since the war have been unique, if for no other reason than that never before in our history has a people enjoyed the mass prosperity found in this country over this period. Is it not logical that a person growing to maturity in the affluent fifties and sixties would be distinguishable from his counterpart who grew up, say, in the depression-ridden 1930s? The question is how will he differ?

Peculiarly, the first reaction to this is usually, "He will be more conservative." This, it seems to me, is just the surface impression. It is alleged that youth today is looking for the easy, secure way. Their goals have changed. Not so many want to be their own boss. Many more want to work for large corporations. Much is made of the fact that youth is security-minded. In the main, this notion seems to derive from surveys which reveal that college graduates, especially, seek positions with large corporations. This propensity toward large corporations grows out of factors other than a quest for security.

How many parents send their sons through college in order that they may open a candy store, a small machine shop, or a real estate office? Very few. By common understanding the topflight college graduates go with topflight institutions. It just seems more glamorous and more appropriate for the senior to seek employment with IBM, RCA, G.M., Du Pont, Scott Paper and the like.

The point is that we are measuring youth by our own standards. These standards are obsolete. The fact of the matter is, it is the competitive, aggressive youth that goes after a job with the large corporation. He knows that he is going to be pitted against the best, and he is willing to face the challenge.

The new adults on the whole will be less security-minded than were the rest of us when we reached that age. Their whole childhood environment will have been spent in or near prosperity. They'll find it easier to believe that there is not going to be another major depression, ever. They will be more inclined to take security for granted than to seek it.

From within this psychological climate there will be more tendency to reach out for a higher plane of living, to set new goals of life attainment. Of course, no one can say exactly what this new plane of living will involve, nor exactly when such a surge in desire will arise.

If the desire for a higher standard of life will be provided by the new adults, will there be the necessary purchasing power to enable such a surge? Surely, there could be. It is difficult, however, to be too optimistic about such an eventuality in the near future.

What is needed for the purchasing power to eventuate is a new feeling of common purpose among business, labor, and government. Experience, however, would indicate that feelings of this kind change more slowly even than laws. Perhaps, if all could come to understand what could be gained, and how little lost, attitude changes would come faster.

Some protestations to the contrary, business and labor basically behave as competitors. This mode of behavior was forged for good reason from past events. But the world has changed. The American business system has changed. Each now really regards the other as vital. Yet, because of virtually inbred rivalry, each takes extreme positions to achieve some advantage in the compromising that is sure to follow. This may sound harmless enough; it isn't. Just as huge corporations have found that everyone gets hurt when they engage in old-fashioned all-out competition, so, too, must business and labor.

Neither business nor labor is operating in an economic world disciplined by an invisible hand of competition which causes its selfish actions to work out for common good. Instead each must in its individual actions assess the potential impact on the public well-being. It is their responsibility to forge an improvised hand of accepted procedure that will guide them almost instinctively in the right direction.

Government has a large role to play in the forming of an effective improvised hand. Too frequently in the past, Republican administrations seemed to say, "What is good for business is good for the country." Democrat administrations obviously favored labor. More recently in the administrations of Dwight D. Eisenhower and the late John F. Kennedy there have been gestures toward objectivity. For the most part, however, "objectivity" has seemed to consist of making concessions in order to achieve ends. There has seemed to be little disposition to indicate what is right, rather the tendency was to find a compromise satisfying each side. Such actions actually encourage selfishness on the part of business and labor to get the best of the inevitable bargain.

All of this is pretty preachy and vague. Permit some oversimplification in order for me to spell out in somewhat more detail what I have in mind.

As a result of moves motivated by self-interest, labor finds itself today receiving high wage rates, and generous fringe benefits. But jobs in industry are not growing. Businessmen have rushed the introduction of laborsaving machinery. Machines do not strike, effect production slowdowns, or demand seniority rights. New men are not being hired except when most pressingly needed. When production rises employers would rather pay overtime than hire new employees with all the fringe benefits attached.

As a result of moves motivated by self-interest, business finds itself today selling at high prices, generating much of its own investment funds, and unable to utilize all its capacity. In some industries prices have been driven to a point where costs—including heavy depreciation schedules and some profit—can be covered at quite low, by historical standards, utilization of capacity levels. This gives business a sense of security, but makes it difficult for the economy as a whole to buy enough to utilize all its capacity.

Perhaps even more serious than the static condition of labor, business and the economy are what we know to be the dynamics of the situation. When economic activity picks up steam and begins moving toward full employment and capacity utilization, labor hikes wage and fringe-payments demands. Business responds by raising prices to cover higher costs including larger depreciation reserves. And the advance is snubbed. Only a few are made quite unhappy. Business is able to make a profit, and those working get higher pay.

Government stands to the side, attempting new refinements in the old techniques of monetary and fiscal policies but really never getting to the heart of the matter. The most skillful manipulations are rewarded with some approbation, but make little real dent in unemployment and excess capacity. New programs, such as job retraining, are installed. All the commotion gives some illusion of action, and satisfies the feeling that "something should be done." Nothing, however, seems really changed.

Labor and business must come to realize that each is too big, too powerful to act small, selfishly. Each should come to understand that actions wholly dominated by self-interest are self-defeating. Labor wins a wage increase and loses potential jobs. Business increases its productive ability and decreases its chances of selling all that it can produce.

Government must come to realize that the really vital economic problems are still solved in the marketplace; that much of its fiscal and monetary juggling is redundant, or, at least, could be eliminated if the market were able to be more effective.

The challenge of the future will be for the American economy to provide the spending to enable a substantial rise in material well-being, and, not incidentally, fully employ its work force. It is my thesis that these goals will go unfulfilled unless labor and business first stop acting as antagonists and begin behaving as though motivated by the public interest.

Assuming this first and steepest step is taken, the rest of the climb to a higher living level should come somewhat more naturally. We are not at or close to an economic state in which only a small proportion of us need work to produce affluence for all. Only under such conditions could we reasonably contemplate giving away additional income to enable the spending and investment necessary for higher living levels. As long as most of us must work, it would seem healthier not to undermine the foundations of our income system by giving substantial payments for not working.

On the other hand, we are in an economic position where not all in the labor force need work to produce enough for a good jump—if not universal affluence—in standards of life. The perplexing question is how to get enough income to those who need not work. The answer that I believe will evolve will be that they will be employed by a process best described—though it won't be so called—as "reasonable featherbedding."

Jobs, in the traditional sense, are not increasing and will not in the future increase fast enough. In the recovery following the 1960 recession it took maybe three or four times as much of an increase in total spending to result in a job as in the mid-1950s. Business and labor, as each becomes less inclined toward self-interest, will come to see the necessity of supplying additional employment. It is imperative, however, that it not be obvious that jobs are being created from whole cloth.

Already this process has taken place on a fairly large scale. Many well-paid corporate executives are working in occupations that hardly existed before the war. To some extent, new methods and processes have necessitated swollen executive ranks. Mostly, however, new corporate titles have come as a kind of subconscious response to the fact that the economy can afford them.

Now, for everyone but the smallest corporation, the personnel department hires and fires instead of division chiefs performing the function. Before 1950 economists were a rarity in private companies; now they are a necessary status symbol. (Anthropologists seem to be replacing them for the company that wants to be unique.) Corporations have men at high levels who spend half or more of their time working for the United Fund and other civic enterprises. "Planning" departments with far-sighted thinkers are quite stylish. Two and three junior executives back up seniors where one filled the bill in the past.

What has happened so far is all to the good. More of the same is in order. The jobs that have come into being have much more dignity, therefore afford more social satisfaction in the world in which we live. Why pay someone to watch a machine half the day when he could be doing something all day that is interesting to him and useful to the corporation?

The "featherbedding" that takes place throughout the economy must seem reasonable; then, of course, it won't be featherbedding. The truly challenging task will be for business to go on creating jobs where need in the traditional sense—more obviously now—does not exist; and to make these jobs seem, and actually turn out to be, socially, perhaps even industrially, useful.

If the featherbedding is transparently just that, it will defeat itself. Those working in jobs will feel no compunction to "put out." The whole quality of life will deteriorate much as if money had been given away.

There is no need for this eventuality, fortunately. Values can be added, work can be made satisfying if good minds are put to the task. If abundance has replaced scarcity, those rising to business leadership in the future will be skilled at maintaining demand at levels sufficient to perpetuate affluence, not those able to produce more with less as in the past. Maintaining demand will involve getting money to those who would be unable to find traditional market jobs. The least upsetting and most socially useful way of doing this will be by conscious effort to "manufacture" socially and industrially useful jobs.

It does now and will in the future come hard for the businessman to admit that jobs have to be created. The fact is, probably for good reason he will not come to acknowledge such a state of affairs. As in the past, however, we can be sure that what he says will not necessarily be in strict conformity with what he is doing.

Index